Camp Granada

Camp Granada

A Music Camp Curriculum
Spaced Out! Theme

Eric Branscome

PUBLISHED IN COOPERATION WITH
THE NATIONAL ASSOCIATION FOR MUSIC EDUCATION

ROWMAN & LITTLEFIELD
Lanham • Boulder • New York • London

Published in cooperation with the National Association for Music Education, 1806 Robert Fulton Drive, Reston, Virginia 20191; nafme.org

Published by Rowman & Littlefield
A wholly owned subsidiary of The Rowman & Littlefield Publishing Group, Inc.
4501 Forbes Boulevard, Suite 200, Lanham, Maryland 20706
www.rowman.com

Unit A, Whitacre Mews, 26-34 Stannary Street, London SE11 4AB, United Kingdom

Copyright © 2017 by Eric Branscome

All rights reserved. No part of this book may be reproduced in any form or by any electronic or mechanical means, including information storage and retrieval systems, without written permission from the publisher, except by a reviewer who may quote passages in a review.

British Library Cataloguing in Publication Information Available

Library of Congress Cataloging-in-Publication Data

Names: Branscome, Eric, 1973- author.
Title: Camp Granada : a music camp curriculum / Eric Branscome.
Description: Lanham : Rowman & Littlefield, [2017]
Identifiers: LCCN 2016049719 (print) | LCCN 2016049742 (ebook) |
  ISBN 9781475829280 (cloth : alk. paper) | ISBN 9781475829297 (pbk. : alk. paper) |
  ISBN 9781475829303 (Electronic)
Subjects: LCSH: School music—Instruction and study—Outlines, syllabi, etc. |
  School music—Instruction and study—Activity programs. |
  Education, Elementary—Activity programs | Music camps.
Classification: LCC MT10 .B87 2017 (print) | LCC MT10 (ebook) | DDC 780.71—dc23
LC record available at https://lccn.loc.gov/2016049719

∞™ The paper used in this publication meets the minimum requirements of American National Standard for Information Sciences—Permanence of Paper for Printed Library Materials, ANSI/NISO Z39.48-1992.

Printed in the United States of America

This book is dedicated to the students, teachers, and parents who
have supported music education by hosting and participating
in Camp Granada over the years.

With very special thanks to the campuses that pilot tested the curriculum:

Austin Peay State University

Department of Music and Community School of the Arts
Eric (Igor) Branscome, *Camp Granada Program Director*
Hope (Tex) Branscome, *Connections Instructor*
Brit (Aria) House, *Connections Instructor*
Daniel (Zoltan) Milner, *Game Time Director*
Kortney (Nanerl) Ross, *Basics Instructor*
Erika (Melody) Sitton, *Chorale Instructor*

East Cheatham Elementary School
Cheatham County School District, Ashland City, TN
Kortney Ross, *Program Director*

Glenellen Elementary School & Northeast Elementary Schools
Clarksville, Montgomery County School System, Clarksville, TN
Daniel Milner and Amanda Holla, *Program Directors*

And finally to my wife, Devyn, and daughters, Hope and Meg,
for their continued support and encouragement.

Contents

PART 1: STARTER KIT   **1**

    Introduction   3

1   Starter Kit   7

2   Camp Songs   37

PART 2: CURRICULUM GUIDE: SPACED OUT! THEME   **57**

3   Chorale   71

4   Basics   85

5   Connections   113

6   Games   137

Part 1

STARTER KIT

Introduction

WHAT IS CAMP GRANADA?

Camp Granada is a different kind of camp that exists wherever there are people who love music and who desire to share that love of music with young children. Its sessions are not held on lake-fronts or wooded hills, but in schools, churches, community music programs, homeschool associations, youth organizations, and civic facilities. Its staff members are local music teachers, parents, and volunteers who come together for the purpose of enriching the lives of children through music education. Its curriculum blends the instructional rigor of formal music learning with the fun, excitement, and life-changing atmosphere of a summer camp.

WHAT PURPOSE DOES IT SERVE?

Music is an integral component of child development, and plants the seeds of creativity and self-expression that children will use throughout their lives. More so, music introduces young children to the tools through which they begin to experience and participate with the world around them. Summer camp is an equally transformative opportunity for young children; for it is at the camp when children begin to accept new challenges, break out of their comfort zones, gain independence, and make memories that last a lifetime. There is no better synergy of the powerful, life-changing opportunities of music and summer camp than Camp Granada.

    The mission of Camp Granada is to provide the highest quality music camp experience in a child-centered environment that encourages participation, stimulates creativity, and focuses on fun. We do not strive to turn young children into Beethovens or Mozarts. It is simply our desire to increase each child's awareness and enjoyment of music, and to instill in each child a desire to continue musical involvement for a lifetime.

WHAT ARE THE BENEFITS OF CAMP GRANADA?

First and foremost, Camp Granada is a music enrichment program intended to instill a life-long love of music in all who participate. It is a curriculum for an elementary music camp, and the administrative resources to begin a program anywhere there is interest. Camp Granada is community engagement, intended to impact music outreach in local organizations and youth programs.

Camp Granada is an out-of-the-ordinary fund-raiser whose proceeds from camper tuition benefit the music program of the hosting organizations. Finally, Camp Granada is a unique opportunity for service learning and career education for local high school and college students who may be considering careers in music or music education, and to prepare for their futures by serving as interns at Camp Granada.

HOW DOES CAMP GRANADA WORK?

If you are interested in bringing Camp Granada to your community, there are a few steps you should take. First, preview the Starter Kit and Curriculum Guide included in this book to determine if you have the facilities, personnel, and instructional materials you will need, or if they might be obtained through cooperation with local schools, churches, or other organizations. It may also be helpful to hold an interest meeting with other teachers, parents, or volunteers who might want to be involved.

Next, if you are affiliated with a school, church, or community organization, you will most likely need to make a formal proposal to your administrator or director. Guidelines for the administrative proposal are included in the starter kit, and a proposal template is available for free download at www.granadamusic.org. After you receive administrative approval, follow the next steps described in the Timeline for Implementation included in the Starter Kit.

The Starter Kit describes the logistical and procedural information for beginning your own program, and contains templates for forms, documents, and promotional materials. Many of the templates are also available in digital format at www.granadamusic.org.

The Curriculum Guide describes the year's camp theme, and includes sequential lesson plans based on the year's theme. Each year's curriculum is pilot tested with elementary children in multiple camp sessions before the instructions are finalized and published. The Curriculum Guide also includes a detailed inventory of materials you will need to implement the lessons and activities.

The Camp Granada curriculum is written to integrate content and skills from across all arts and academic disciplines through hands-on learning activities. Concepts and skills are introduced and developed through activity-based lessons where campers benefit from direct application of lesson materials. Lessons usually include singing, instruments, listening activities, movement, art, and creative thinking. The week culminates in a performance for family and friends, for campers to demonstrate the skills and concepts they have learned through the week. Each year a new curriculum guide describes lessons and activities related to the yearly camp theme.

GOOD LUCK!

A Camp Granada program in your community will be an incredibly rewarding experience for all who participate. The time, effort, and energy you expend to organize the program will be returned to you tenfold as you see the musical and social development of the children who participate, and you will not regret your decision to host Camp Granada in your community.

Chapter 1

Starter Kit

The Starter Kit is your survival guide to prepare for and manage all of the administrative duties of hosting a session of Camp Granada. The kit provides a suggested timeline for implementation and contains templates for all of the documents and forms that you will need, most of which are available in customizable digital format at www.granadamusic.org. Following the timelines, guidelines, and procedural suggestions in the Starter Kit should ensure successful program implementation, and minimize or eliminate any surprises along the way.

ADMINISTRATIVE PROPOSAL

Usually, the first step of implementing Camp Granada is to obtain the approval of the campus administrator. Although not all administrators will pose the same questions, there is some degree of consistency regarding the types of information that administrators will need to know. Most information for a thorough administrative proposal has been included in the Starter Kit and is available as a free PDF at www.granadamusic.org. There are some program- and facility-specific considerations you should make before proposing Camp Granada to your administrator. Generally, the administrative proposal should include the following.

Program Overview

Prepare an overview of the essential information to describe Camp Granada to your administrator. It may help to summarize the following sections of the Starter Kit:

- What is Camp Granada?
- What purpose does it serve?
- How will it benefit the hosting organization?
- How does Camp Granada work?
- What will I need to provide as the facility administrator?

Facilities

Preview the *Facilities and Scheduling* section of the Starter Kit to evaluate how Camp Granada will best function on your campus, and determine what rooms will be needed.

Finances

Preview the *Financial Information* section of the Starter Kit and make some preliminary considerations for your camp session based on your program needs and local economy. Mainly, you will need to determine how much you plan to charge campers for tuition and how much you plan to pay staff, or if you plan to recruit staff as volunteers. It is also helpful to project a minimum to maximum enrollment, how much net and gross income you predict, and decide how your music department will spend the revenue gained through Camp Granada.

Personnel

Preview the *Personnel Needs* section of the Starter Kit and make a tentative list of local teachers, parents, or other people you plan to recruit as camp staff.

Safety and Security

Preview the *Camp Policies* section of the Starter Kit and determine how the included information fits into the policies already in place on your campus.

TIMELINE FOR IMPLEMENTATION

This timeline provides a skeletal outline to implement a Camp Granada program. It is designed to help you stay on target, complete the required tasks in a timely manner, and manage the numerous administrative details of hosting a camp program. Additional guidelines and procedures are included in the remainder of the Starter Kit.

About Six Months to a Year before the Program

- Hold an interest meeting to discuss the possibility of Camp Granada at your facility. Invite the people whom you might consider asking to work as staff or serve as volunteers, the parents of potential campers, and administrators who will eventually need to approve the program.
- Obtain approval from your campus administrator, system supervisor, or other administrative personnel.
- Communicate with administrators to determine dates for your camp session.
- Ensure that no summer maintenance will occur in the rooms you will need during the week of camp.
- Ensure lights and air-conditioning will be on during the desired week of camp.
- Ensure rooms will be unlocked and available, or make sure that you will be given the keys.
- Determine if you will have custodial staff or if you will be responsible for emptying trash, cleaning floors, or replacing restroom supplies.
- Begin to create documents (posters and flyers) that will be used to promote your program and recruit campers and staff. A reproducible template for each year's theme is available at www.granadamusic.org.

Three to Six Months in Advance

Finalize dates with your hosting organization.

- Distribute promotional materials and begin recruiting campers.
- Familiarize yourself with your hosting organization's financial policies. This will determine how money is collected, how workers are paid, and how supplies are purchased.
- Begin to recruit and hire camp staff and volunteers.
- Create camp policies and guidelines for your program (suggestions are included the Starter Kit).
- Monitor ongoing camper enrollment and income, and send confirmation letters to campers as they enroll.

One to Three Months in Advance

As money becomes available, begin to order, purchase, or compile instructional supplies.

- Begin to prepare instructional and administrative supplies.
- If possible, distribute lesson plans and songs to camp staff so that they can begin learning the songs and other materials.

In the Weeks Prior to Camp

- Ensure camp staff have all instructional materials and have begun preparing.
- Order camp T-shirts using the graphics provided on the CD—www.granadamusic.org (optional).
- Assemble leader notebooks (see the *Leader Training* section of the Starter Kit for more information).
- As the enrollment cut-off date approaches
  - Determine the number of teams and classes you will need
  - Assign campers to teams and classes
  - Make team and class rosters
  - Make camper and leader name tags
  - Meet with camp staff for leader training (see the *Leader Training* section of the Starter Kit for more information).

About One Week Prior to Camp

- Sort and prepare T-shirts for distribution (optional).
- Sort and prepare camper name tags for distribution.
- As rooms become available
  - Begin to set up classrooms and instructional materials
  - Begin to decorate as needed

Opening Day

- Post signs around your facility, directing parents to the right doors for check in.
- Ensure all appropriate doors are unlocked, lights are on, and the facility is ready for camp.
- Double check all rooms to ensure instructional supplies are prepped and ready for use.

Each Day of Camp

- Ensure all appropriate doors are unlocked, lights are on, and the facility is ready for camp.
- Prepare any instructional materials that are needed for the day's lessons and activities (this task may be completed by individual instructors).

Closing Day

- The final day of camp requires attention to a few extra details that will ensure the success of the closing ceremony, and will close out your camp without any loose ends.
    - Prior to the start of the final day, move all instruments from the Basics and Chorale rooms to the performance area and set it up for the performance. Also setup choral risers if you are using them for your program.
    - Create, print, and copy programs for your closing ceremony (optional). Additional program information is available in the Starter Kit. A list of performance selections in program order is provided in the introduction to each curriculum guide. Finally, theme-based program templates and logos are available at www.granadamusic.org.
    - Prepare team prizes or treats in advance and set them aside to distribute after the closing ceremony (optional).
    - As campers are finishing lunch on the final day, allow a suitable amount of time for campers (or staff or interns) to move all art projects (completed or otherwise) from the art area to the cafeteria or dismissal area.
    - An ideal dismissal: At the end of camp, it is important that everyone leaves with all of their belongings, and a well-planned dismissal can facilitate this process. At the end of the closing ceremony, announce that campers will return to the cafeteria (dismissal area) where they can retrieve their lunch boxes, art projects, and their end-of-the-week: As you dismiss, lead campers to the cafeteria and ensure they get all their belongings before they are signed out.

After Camp

- The usual camp rule is to leave a camp site in better condition than it was when you arrived. Clean every room you used, ensuring all furniture and equipment are returned to their original places.
- Ensure everything is returned to its original location and all camp materials are packed and ready for next year.
- Type and send a thank-you letter to administrators who approved your program, staff, and campers. Be sure to include an invitation to next year's program to boost enrollment for your next session. It is also a good gesture to prepare a certificate to present to your staff on the final day of camp.
- Submit financial documents, ensure all invoices are paid, and thats all staff receive their payment (if needed).
- If your program was run as a fund-raiser, send the check or equipment to the appropriate parties or purchase supplies for which the funds were intended.

- Send a follow-up press release to your local newspaper or social media to generate excitement about your next session.

PERSONNEL NEEDS

One of the highest priorities for ensuring a successful Camp Granada program is recruiting camp staff that will work cohesively, generate a positive camp environment, and lead activities effectively.

Program Director

The program director is responsible for administering Camp Granada, and serves as the primary point of contact between the community and the hosting organization. The program director monitors incoming enrollment, collects tuition money, orders supplies, and trains the leaders and other volunteers. The program director also deals with more significant behavioral or medical issues that may arise during the camp. The program director may teach one or more of the classes, lead games, or fulfill other duties, based on the size of the program. This person needs to be someone who is very detail and task oriented. Usually one program director is suitable, or two who can work cohesively.

Teachers

The teachers are directly responsible for delivering lessons to the children. While it is not necessary for the teachers to be licensed music educators, they do need to be skilled in communicating with young children in a musical context. The number of teachers you will need is based on the size of your program (roughly one class for every ten to fifteen campers and one teacher per class). Usually, teachers are needed in the following areas.

Chorale (Singing)

One teacher will lead small- and large-group singing, teach songs and singing skills, and prepare campers for the singing portion of the closing ceremony.

Basics (Instruments and Music Literacy)

One teacher is needed to teach basic music theory and use of pitched and non-pitched (Orff) instruments, and prepare the instrumental portion of the closing ceremony.

Connections (Arts and Movement)

One teacher will lead arts and crafts activities, and occasionally lead movement, or instrument-based activities.

Game Director

The game director is responsible for leading games with all campers. Since the games are kinesthetic, Physical Education (PE) style activities, it is helpful if the game director is somewhat athletic. It is also important for the game director to have a working knowledge of music, and to be able to manage larger groups of children. Usually, a camp session has one game director, and sometimes one intern who helps primarily with games.

Team Leaders

Team leaders sit with their assigned teams at lunch and help team members during afternoon game time, primarily following the instructions of the game director. Team leaders may be interns, teachers, or additional staff members who serve solely in the capacity of team leader. (You will need roughly one team for every 10 to 12 children and one leader per team.)

Interns

Many high schools, churches, and youth clubs require its members to fulfill volunteer hours each year. Camp Granada is a perfect opportunity for high school musicians who may be considering careers in music education to fulfill their volunteer hours. Interns may serve as team leaders, instructional aides, or general assistants for some administrative tasks. It is helpful to have approximately one intern per team and, if needed, additional interns to help in game time, and/or administrative tasks.

Where to Find Camp Staff?

Usually the hosting organization (music school, church, etc.) employs people to work with young musicians who may be suitable Camp Granada teachers or team leaders. Camp Granada may also be implemented as a joint effort of 2 or more elementary schools utilizing the teaching staff from those schools as camp staff. You may offer tuition discounts or waivers to parents of children who want to attend camp, if they volunteer to serve a certain number of hours, or the entire week.

Local colleges are also excellent resources for finding qualified music and music education majors to work as camp staff. Finally, students in high school music programs may be suitable Camp Granada interns. It is recommended that each Camp Granada worker completes a criminal background check, or follows standard protocol of the hosting organization for anyone wishing to work with minors.

FINANCIAL INFORMATION

As you continue the process of preparing to host Camp Granada, you will need to consider how finances will be managed. Financial policies and guidelines are described below. They may be modified to adhere to any preexisting guidelines that may already be in place at your hosting organization.

How Much Does It Cost to Run a Week of Camp?

Camp Granada can function on a wide range of budgets, based on the number of campers, paid or volunteer staff, and the extravagance of decorations, team prizes, and other nonessentials. While many of the nonessentials do not have any bearing on the quality of instruction, they do contribute to the overall image of camp presented to the campers and parents, and should be considered as the budget is formulated. Start-up costs are minimal and are usually limited to office supplies needed to create and distribute promotional materials.

Materials, equipment, and other supplies are usually purchased with money collected from tuition and fees. These costs usually include the following:

- Building or facility usage for one week
- Office supplies for instructional materials
- Custodial staff (may not be required if Camp Granada staff agree to manage cleaning tasks for the week)
- Camp staff compensation (see below for options)
- Art and craft supplies (ask for donations or borrow equipment from other organizations to reduce costs)
- Instructional materials and equipment that are not already available (try to borrow equipment from other organizations to reduce costs)
- Camper prizes for the closing ceremony (optional)

How Much Should I Charge for Tuition?

The primary consideration for camp tuition is the economic status of your local community. Tuition should be substantial enough to pay for the required materials and staff to manage the program, but should not be so high that it becomes prohibitive for children in the community. Typically, camp tuition should range from $50 to $75 per camper.

Other options to consider include the following:

- Provide discounted or waived tuition for campers whose parents or guardians volunteer to serve in some capacity.
- Offer discounts for families with multiple children ($75 for the first child and $50 for each additional sibling).
- If your program will provide camp shirts, consider $50 tuition plus the cost of a shirt for campers who wish to purchase one (approximately $10–$15), or $75 tuition that includes a shirt for every camper.

How Should Workers Be Compensated?

1. There are several important factors to consider when determining compensation for staff, and these considerations will be made by the program director, in cooperation with the hosting organization's administrator. If your hosting organization is already set up to pay employees and deal with appropriate tax records, this may be the most suitable format to pay camp staff. If you choose to pay staff, consider one of two options: Pay each staff member a flat or hourly rate. In this format, you need to have a suitable number of campers and charge enough tuition to pay staff.
2. Pay each staff member based on the number of campers who enroll. This may encourage staff to recruit more campers to your program.

Other Forms of Compensation

Compensation for workers may also come in the form of a donation to each worker's school if your staff members are music teachers who need supplies for their programs.

Also consider offering volunteer service points in exchange for working at a camp session. This has already been discussed for high school interns, but may also be suitable for college students or adults who are involved in civic or religious organizations that require community service.

An Ideal Budget

An ideal budget should be generated early in the process of organizing a camp program. This budget will then help you decide a minimum to maximum range of campers to enroll, the number of staff to recruit, whether or not to purchase or borrow instructional equipment, cost for tuition and fees, and other decisions that impact profit. As a general guideline, an ideal budget may include the following (table 1.1).

Table 1.1 Budget Estimates

Expenses	Lowest Range	Highest Range
Staff compensation	25% (of income)	40% (of income)
Instructional materials	15%	20%
Office and promotional supplies	5%	10%
(T-shirts)—optional	0%	20%
Facility use or rental	0%	10%
Profit	55%	0%

Camp Shirts

The cost for camp shirts should be paid by campers, either with camp tuition, or as an additional and optional fee for those who wish to purchase a shirt. While T-shirts are a nonessential part of camp, they do contribute to the overall camp environment for participants, create a heightened image of professionalism for your organization, and can serve as a useful marketing tool as children wear your shirts throughout the year, promoting your program in the local community. Templates and graphics files are available for download at www.granadamusic.org.

Start-Up Costs

The first summer you host a session of Camp Granada, there will be more start-up expenses than usual. However, these costs can be minimized through creative planning, researching grants, requesting donations, or by using materials already available to you. Costs can also be minimized by borrowing instructional instruments and equipment, or through establishing partnerships with local music businesses or programs.

Fund-Raising Tip

If you are going to use Camp Granada as a fund-raiser for your program, it may be helpful to decide exactly how profits will be used, and include a statement of intent on your promotional materials.

Examples:

All proceeds will be used to purchase _____ (equipment) for the music classroom

All proceeds will be used to pay for a music field trip to_____ (location)

CAMPER INFORMATION

As you consider budget, facilities, and the number of staff members to recruit, you will also need to consider program enrollment. Campers typically include children ranging from age 5, having completed kindergarten, through 11, having completed 5th grade. While some younger children may be ready for a camp environment, it is most helpful if every camper has completed kindergarten so they will be able to function in a class environment.

The number of campers may vary based on your facilities, equipment, and the number of helpers available to you. There needs to be a sufficient number of campers for everyone to experience the ensemble format of some of the lessons, and the team competition of the game time activities, but not so many campers that the program becomes unmanageable. Typically, the suitable number of campers ranges from 20 to 50. If you have more than 50 children interested in camp, consider holding consecutive sessions of camp and limiting enrollment in each week.

How to Divide Campers

Once your registration deadline has passed and you know the ages and genders of the children that are coming to camp, campers should be divided for morning instructional activities by age or grade, with approximately 10–15 campers per class. You will need to consider the number of children and their ages to determine the most suitable division. The early elementary lessons are usually suitable for 5-, 6-, or 7-year-olds. The middle elementary lessons are suitable for 7-, 8-, or 9-year-olds. And the upper elementary lessons are suitable for 9–11-year-olds.

In smaller programs, you can divide children into two groups (ages 5–8 and 9–11) and then modify the curriculum by choosing sections from the middle elementary lesson materials that you may want to perform with the older or younger groups.

For game time, campers should be divided by teams with an equal number of campers per team, and an equal number of youngest and oldest campers. Sometimes, parents request a camp buddy for their child, another camper with whom their child wants to be paired. When organizing teams, ensure that all camp buddies are grouped together as this increases the likelihood that every child will enjoy the camp experience.

To boost a sense of team spirit, use team colors (red, blue, yellow, green), and/or allow each team to select a team name or mascot. Campers sit by teams at lunch and at the camper showcase, and usually stand by teams in the large-group singing portion of the closing ceremony.

Once campers are divided by age for morning activities, and into teams for lunch and games, you will need to create rosters that you will distribute to your staff to ensure every child is in the correct team and class. A sample roster will have name, age, gender, team color, and camp buddy for each camper.

If you have a larger program (sixty or more campers), consider one of two options: Either hold an additional week of camp and try to evenly divide campers between the two weeks or, if you only have one week available, divide your campers into younger and older campers. Send your younger campers to classes in the morning and games in the afternoon, and send your older campers to games in the morning and classes in the afternoon. This model is equivalent of holding two simultaneous camp sessions with reversed schedules.

FACILITIES AND SCHEDULING

Usually, facilities and scheduling are closely related as room availability may determine when you are able to offer certain classes. Similarly, the number of campers involved in your program may determine where certain activities are located. As a guideline, facility needs typically include the following:

- Base camp: A central meeting location for the opening and closing session. Some classes may also meet at base camp.
- Cafeteria: A suitable facility with tables and chairs for campers to eat lunch.
- Classroom space: One room is needed for each class in your program. Ideally, rooms should be free of desks or chairs, and have enough room for rehearsal, instruction, and movement. The connections room should have a tiled or linoleum floor and enough tables and chairs for each camper to work.
- Game/activity room: Game time is typically held in a large room or small gymnasium. If weather permits and the games are modified to fit the conditions, game time may be held outdoors.
- Stage: A large performance space for the closing ceremony. A gymnatorium or cafetorium may serve multiple camp purposes.

Daily Schedule

Camp Granada is typically a five-hour day that begins with small-group instruction and ends with large-group activities. The number of classes

Table 1.2 Typical Schedule

Time	Session	Location
8:45–9:00 a.m.	Pre-Session	Base Camp
9:00–9:20	Welcome Session	Base Camp
9:30–10:15	Break Out Session 1	Classrooms
10:20–11:05	Break Out Session 2	Classrooms
11:10–11:55	Break Out Session 3	Classrooms
12:00–12:30	Lunch	Cafeteria
12:30–1:00	Camper Showcase	Cafeteria, Base Camp, or Stage
1:00–1:45	Game Time	Gymnasium
1:45–2:00	Coda Session	Base Camp
2:00	Dismissal	Base Camp

you need depends on the size of your program and availability of facilities. Table 1.2 shows a model Camp Granada schedule.

Table 1.3 Breakout Session Rotation

	Early Elementary	Middle Elementary	Upper Elementary
Breakout Session 1	Chorale	Connections	Basics
Breakout Session 2	Basics	Chorale	Connections
Breakout Session 3	Connections	Basics	Chorale

In the breakout sessions, you will need to generate a rotation to accommodate the size of your program. Examples are in table 1.3.

This model assumes a larger group of campers (40 or more) where students are divided into three instructional groups for breakout sessions (youngest, middle ages, oldest). A smaller program may only divide campers into two instructional groups and may need to modify the schedule (table 1.4).

Table 1.4 Schedule for Smaller Programs

8:45–9:00 a.m.	Pre-Session	Base camp
9:00–9:20	Welcome Session	Base camp
9:30–10:20	Breakout Session 1	Classrooms
10:30–11:20	Breakout Session 2	Classrooms
11:30–12:00	Lunch	Cafeteria
12:00–12:30	Camper Showcase	Cafeteria, base camp, or stage
12:30–1:00	Large Group Singing	Cafeteria, base camp, or stage
1:00–1:45	Game Time	Gymnasium
1:45–2:00	Coda Session	Base camp
2:00	Dismissal	Base camp

The primary difference in these two schedules is based on the group-singing session. Children are more likely to participate in singing activities when there are more people singing at a time. In larger camp programs, singing can be placed in the morning sessions when the campers are divided by age, and the teaching can be more directly targeted to the various age groups.

In smaller camp programs, it is more favorable to teach singing through large-group instruction in the afternoon time. This is accomplished by moving lunch earlier in the day and teaching singing in a large-group format. In either schedule format, allow a 5- to 10-minute transition between activities for campers to visit the restroom or get a drink, and to allow teachers to reset for the next group.

What to Expect in each Activity Time

Each daily activity should be designed to fulfill its unique needs and to provide a seamless flow from one activity to another. Typical activity sessions include the following:

Opening day check in *(first day only)*. Camp doors open earlier than normal to allow for opening day check in. Parents complete a check-in form, are introduced to their child's team leader and walk their children to base camp. Parents may play games with their child until the start of camp.

Pre-session. Organize board games, card games, coloring sheets, or other low-key activities to welcome children to camp and allow for interaction among campers and between campers and staff. Music board game suggestions are included in *Music Board Game Workshop* by Eric Branscome (available from Alfred Publications).

Welcome session. The first session of the day includes time for skits and announcements, and other pertinent information campers need to know about the day. The welcome session also has camp songs and movement activities, and may include a brief time of stretching to prepare for the day.

Breakout sessions. These are the primary instructional sessions where most music content is learned, and students rehearse materials for the closing ceremony. All lessons are contained in the Curriculum Guide. Campers are divided by age and rotated through two to three stations, depending on program size: (1) Basics (instruments and music reading), (2) Chorale (singing), and (3) Connections (art and movement). In smaller programs, singing can be scheduled as large-group choir rehearsal in the afternoon.

Lunch. Staff sit with campers, and campers sit by teams to encourage social interaction among teammates.

Camper showcase. Many children are involved in piano, voice, dance, or other lessons and may enjoy an opportunity to perform for their friends in a low-stress, no-competition environment. Camp staff or guest artists are also encouraged to perform. The camper showcase is also a 30-minute time of physical rest before game time. A blank on the registration form asks parents to indicate if their child would like to participate in the camper showcase. Once all campers have registered, the program director will need to organize a camper showcase rotation based on the number of children who signed up.

If there are not enough campers who have signed up for the showcase, fill this time with group singing, skits, and other camp-related activities. You can also use these skits to teach children how to perform, how to be in an audience, introduce them to new music, and countless other music-related lessons.

Afternoon Game time. Camp Granada games are kinesthetic and energetic. Incorporate musical skills and concepts from the morning lessons. All games are described in the Curriculum Guide. Campers are grouped by teams and they earn points through sportsmanship and winning games.

Coda session. The camp day ends with a time for any announcements campers may need to know for the following day. Campers should also clean up, gather personal items, and prepare for dismissal.

Dismissal. Parents sign out children from base camp, gather belongings, and go home. Campers are invited to play games from the morning session to stay occupied while they wait for parents/guardians to sign them out.

Closing ceremony *(final day only)*. The camp week concludes with a sharing time for campers to demonstrate what they have learned through the week to friends and family. At the end of the performance, the final team points are revealed and the winning team receives its prize.

CAMP POLICIES

One of the last preparatory steps is to create a set of enforceable policies for your session of Camp Granada. You may use the policies that are already in place at your hosting organization, copy and customize the policy suggestions described below, or create your own policies that best suit the needs of your program. Policies should be posted on your organization's website, or made available to parents and campers on a registration packet or confirmation letter. Sample policies and policy wording include the following:

What to Bring

- Lunch. Campers will not have access to the vending machines.
- Water bottle (optional) with your child's name clearly labeled.
- Materials for camper showcase (optional).

What not to Bring

- Toys, cell phones, iPods, or any other device that is not permitted at school.
- Unregistered friends or relatives of campers may not attend camp.
- **We are not responsible for lost, stolen, or broken items that campers choose to bring to camp.*

Camper Code of Conduct

The mission of Camp Granada can only be achieved when campers and counselors work together in an environment of mutual respect. Therefore, campers are held accountable to certain behavioral standards. Fighting, stealing, bullying, and disrespect of camp staff or fellow campers will not be tolerated. Significant or consistent discipline problems may cause campers to be sent home. The camp director will determine if and when a child should return. No refunds will be given for campers who are sent home for disciplinary reasons.

General Rules and Policies

- Campers should only go in parts of the building reserved for Camp Granada.
- Campers should go to restrooms in pairs (not wander the halls alone).
- Approximately 10 minutes has been provided between sessions rather than during sessions for campers to use the restroom.
- Campers should always walk while inside any building on campus.

Dismissal Time

Camp ends promptly at 2:00 p.m. All campers should be picked up no later than 2:15 out of respect for camp staff who usually have afternoon commitments. If you pick up your child after 2:15 for more than 2 consecutive days, your child may be dismissed from camp or you will be charged an additional fee of $ _____ (amount).

At the end of each day, you will sign out your camper at the tables in the _____ (location). We want to ensure that each child returns home safely so please remember to sign out. Children will only be dismissed to people whose names were included on the registration form.

Medical Information

Prescribed and non-prescribed medications may only be administered by campers' parents or guardians. If your camper requires medication during camp hours, please come at the appropriate time to administer the medication. Campers may bring inhalers but not with any other medication. In the event there is a medical emergency during camp hours, the directors will call 911 first and then notify you. Please let us know if your child is allergic to any foods, latex balloons, or other elements to which he/she may be exposed during camp.

Please do not bring any child who is ill or has a related contagious ailment (lice, pink eye, etc.). Generally, children should be fever free for 24 hours to participate in the Camp Granada. If your child becomes ill or is injured during Camp Granada, you will receive an incident report to let you know what happened and how the situation was handled.

In the Event of an Emergency

Medical issues. No medication of any kind (including topical ointments) may be distributed by a camp counselor. Each classroom has access to a basic first-aid kit for minor cuts and scrapes (adhesive bandages only). Camp staff will complete an incident report anytime there is a related medical issue. For medical emergencies, staff will immediately contact the camp director who will then call 911 and the parent/guardians of campers who were involved.

Behavioral issues. Camp staff will handle minor behavioral issues as needed. Staff will complete an incident report for repeated or major behavioral issues. Staff will contact the camp director if assistance is needed (especially when a camper's behavior threatens the physical or emotional safety of yourself or another camper).

Stranger danger. If a suspicious person is seen on campus, staff will call the camp director immediately, and do not allow any children to leave the activity area.

Weather-related emergencies. In the event of a weather-related emergency, Camp Granada should follow the hosting organization's standard procedure. Camp staff should quickly and quietly bring all campers to the pre-designated storm shelter.

Fire. If the building's fire alarm sounds, camp staff will take their groups to the nearest exit and await further instructions.

LEADER TRAINING

Shortly before your opening day of camp, you will need to host a leader-training session. Prior to the training session, leaders should have received lesson materials from the Curriculum Guide and begun preparing to teach in their assigned area. The training session should address the following areas.

General Information

- Arrival and dismissal time: Leaders need to know when and where to report, and when they will be able to leave at the end of the day.
- Roles and responsibilities: Each staff member should be hired with a specific job in mind. Prior to the start of the session, staff will also need to know about the other duties as assigned aspects of their duties.
- Dress code: Staff need to know what to wear and what to avoid wearing. This may be determined by your host organization or program director.
- What to Bring: Staff need to know what specific items to bring or avoid bringing.

Titles

Each staff member will need to determine how he or she wants to be addressed by the campers. In some programs, it is perfectly acceptable to have campers address staff with formal titles (Mr. or Mrs. last name). In other circumstances, children are more accustomed to the informality of Mr. or Mrs. first name. You may also use camp nicknames as a compromise between the risk of too formal and too informal. Encourage staff members to pick a nickname—something related to music—and determine what they want children to learn from their nickname.

Atmosphere

Any event, program, or organization will only be as successful as the people in charge, and the ability of those people to work as a cohesive team. This is especially true in a camp environment, or anywhere that children are involved. Therefore, it is essential for Camp Granada directors, staff, and interns to work as a unified entity, and to generate a friendly, welcoming, and encouraging environment where children will feel at ease, and will be willing to participate.

To instill this spirit from the first meeting of the staff, it may be helpful to begin with an icebreaker activity that will demonstrate and illustrate the need for staff members to work as a team. Spend a few minutes introducing everyone, especially interns and first-time workers who may feel out of place. Share your goals and aspirations for the program, and the vital role that staff will play in the achievement of those goals.

Facilities

Ensure all staff members are well acquainted with the facilities. Make sure everyone knows where the children's and adult's restrooms are located, where children will arrive and be dismissed, where to find each activity room, any parts of the building that are off-limits to campers, and where to find essential equipment (e.g., first-aid kit). Also, ensure that all staff members know the procedural expectations for campers in each activity room. This is especially important regarding any safety concerns that may be related to your facilities.

Daily Schedule and Rotation

All staff should be aware of the daily schedule and course rotation. Ensure your leader training provides an overview of the schedule, and outlines specific duties and responsibilities for each staff member throughout the day.

Camper Code of Conduct

Behavioral expectations should be communicated to staff, parents of campers, and to the campers. During staff training, make sure staff know how to manage off-task behaviors and the procedures in place for your program. This discussion is especially important for interns, or younger workers with little or no prior experience. Should you choose to use an incident report form, ensure that your staff know how to complete the form and what to do with it once it is submitted (a template for the incident report form is available in the *Administrative Extras* section of the Starter Kit and at www.granadamusic.org).

Necessary Evils

One of the most desirable attributes for teachers is that of integrity. Parents want to know that they are entrusting their most prized possessions to only the most trustworthy people. While professional teachers have been taught how to deal with children, some high school interns and college students who have not yet taken teacher-training courses will need a brief overview of appropriate ways to interact with children.

This is especially important in dealing with off-task behaviors, managing restroom time, and addressing appropriate touch. As general guidelines for those who have not had formal training, do not do anything that would make a parent question your integrity or that would put you in an unfavorable situation:

- Do not allow yourself to be alone in a room with a child or small group of children.
- Do not use the same restrooms that the campers use, especially when campers are in the restroom.
- Do not allow children to sit in your lap.
- Use side hugs rather than front hugs.
- Do not try to handle behavioral issues that are beyond your comfort level.

In the Event of an Emergency

Prior to the start of camp, the program director should research the emergency-readiness policies of the host organization, and/or generate new policies where there is a need (examples have been included in the *Camp Policies* section of the Starter Kit). These procedures need to be communicated to the parents of your campers so that they will know that their children will be protected, what to expect in case of an emergency, and how extreme medical or behavioral issues will be managed.

Camp Songs and Traditions

The most memorable parts of a camp experience for most children stem from the camp songs, traditions, and random acts of humor that give each camp its own unique personality, and contribute to the camp's atmosphere of fun. Make sure your staff know the songs that you plan to use in the opening ceremony, or any additional skits and activities you plan to implement throughout the week.

Team Sports

For games, campers are divided into teams and teams compete in PE-style games for points that are collected throughout the week. Although points are earned through team competition, this aspect of Camp Granada is not in any way to be emphasized over learning. Camp Granada should not become an overly competitive environment where points are the primary focus. Staff will need to be prepared to deal with overly competitive campers, and to instill the concept of sportsmanship, regardless of the score.

Team points can also be a powerful motivator for good behavior and sportsmanship. For example, extra team points may be awarded to:

- The first team to get quiet when asked
- The first team to line up for activities
- The team whose table looks the cleanest after lunch
- Teams who demonstrate the most team spirit during games (even when their team is losing)
- A team member who demonstrates integrity, character, or respect to another team member or team leader.

Finally, it is helpful if staff have been exposed to some of the Camp Granada games before the start of camp. Although this is not essential, it will prepare them to assist the game director more effectively. If you have enough time in your training session, allow your game director to lead staff through some of the games as you talk through some of the related game rules.

Camp Theme and Lesson Content

Finally, the staff will need an overview of the camp theme, lesson content, and how each staff member's role contributes to the overall program. This will enable the staff to illustrate connections between the singing lesson, the craft project for the day, and games. In addition, this will be especially important in the final days of the program when classes are brought together as campers prepare for the closing ceremony.

LEADER NOTEBOOK

Each staff member should be provided with a leader notebook including:

- An outline of the topics addressed in leader training
- Music and/or lyrics for camp songs for staff to learn before the start of camp
- A roster showing the names of all children attending camp. The roster should also provide each child's age and team color so that all children can be accounted for during all parts of the day.
- Lesson materials: Each staff member should have a hard copy of the lesson materials he or she is responsible for teaching.
- Scratch pad, legal pad, or spare notebook paper
- Pencil pouch including: extra pens or pencils, blank incident report forms, small bottle of hand sanitizer, and Band-Aids

ADMINISTRATIVE EXTRAS

This section of the Starter Kit describes additional elements of Camp Granada that are not necessarily essential, but do help you organize your session, and contribute to a successful program.

Promotional Flyer

One of the most essential documents for a successful camp program is your promotional flyer or poster. This flyer will be your main source of promoting your program, generating awareness in the community, and recruiting campers. It should be visually captivating as much as it is informative. Sample flyer templates are available at www.granadamusic.org. If you design your own flyer, be sure it includes:

- Logo and theme: Include a large Camp Granada logo and logo of the annual theme.
- Fonts: The usual Camp Granada font is Kristen ITC, available on most computers, or for free download from various websites. Additional fonts based on each year's theme are described in the introduction to the Curriculum Guide.
- Program description: Especially in your first year, the community may not be aware of Camp Granada and will need a general description of the program. Copy and paste sections of the administrative proposal to generally describe Camp Granada, the types of classes it entails, and the benefits

of the program. Close this section with a general description of the year's theme (located in the annual Curriculum Guide)
- Dates/times/location: Include the days and times of your program (start to end), and where your program will be located.
- Target audience: Include ages or grades that you will include in your program.
- Registration: Include information describing where parents should go to register their child(ren).
- Cost: Include the cost per child and if you plan to include any multi-child discounts, early-bird registration discounts, or other related incentives.
- Contact: Include name and contact information of program director, or other primary point of contact for your program.

Registration Form

A thorough, yet concise registration form should gather as much information as possible, in a format that is easy for parents to complete. A registration template is available at www.granadamusic.org. If your hosting organization does not have a standard registration form, or if you choose to make your own registration form or website, be sure it includes:

- Contact information: First and last name and contact information of parents/guardians (address, home phone, cell phone).
- Emergency contact information: In case of an emergency who, other than the parent/guardian should be contacted.
- For each child: First and last name, gender, age or grade, T-shirt size (optional), and birthday (optional). The form should allow families to register more than one child, or should specify "please complete one registration form for each child you wish to enroll."
- Pick-up information: Spaces for parents/guardians to indicate who is authorized to pick up their child(ren).
- Payment information: The form should be very clear regarding payment information:
  - How much is due
  - What types of payments are acceptable
  - To whom should checks be written
  - To what address should payments be sent
  - What is the payment deadline
  - What is the late fee and deadline for late registration
- Camper showcase information: Fields for parents/guardians to list title, composer, and performance medium (instrument/voice) for any child wishing to participate in the camper showcase (optional).

- Camp buddy: Fields for parents/guardians to list other campers with whom their child wants to be grouped (optional).
- Medical insurance number: If your organization requires, you will need to obtain the name of the parent/guardian's insurance provider and policy number in the event of an emergency. In lieu of this on the form, you may copy the insurance card at opening day check in (optional).
- Acknowledgment and consent: A statement that indicates parent/guardian submission of the registration form acknowledges they have read and agreed to comply with all camp policies (optional).
- Photo or press release: If you intend to take pictures or video record your event, you will need parental consent of each child in order to use the pictures in future promotional materials (optional).
- *Example*: I authorize (name of organization) to use my child's picture for Camp Granada promotional materials including printed and online photographs, video and audio recordings of Camp Events, and written articles describing my child's participation in Camp Granada. I understand that I will not receive royalties or other form of compensation for the use of my child's picture or other representation.

Confirmation Letter

Every parent who enrolls in camp should receive a confirmation letter or e-mail. This lets parents know you have received their registration, and provides additional information they will need to prepare for camp. The confirmation letter should include:

- Names: Name of child(ren) who were registered
- Payment information: Either a receipt of payment, or a notice of payment due
- Camp policies (what to bring, what not to bring, etc.)
- Schedule: When to arrive in the morning, and what time to pick up in the afternoon
- Location: Be as specific as you can, especially if your camp program is in a large facility. Let parents know specifically where to park, which doors will be unlocked, and how to get to the check-in location.
- Miscellaneous: There may be additional information unique to your program that parents will need to know before the first day of camp.

Name Tags

Especially on the first day of camp, provide a name tag for all staff and campers. If your program is open to an entire community, there is a strong probability that many children will not know each other or the camp staff.

Name tags will help you learn the campers' names more quickly and will help parents and campers identify camp staff.

Sign In and Sign Out

Consider some type of sign-in and sign-out procedures. This will not only ensure accurate attendance record and confirm that all children go home with the right person, but it will also present an image of safety and organization to the parents of your program. For the sign-in procedure, have all of your camper name tags available on a check-in table, monitored by a staff member. You will be able to track attendance simply by looking for leftover name tags once the day begins. For the sign-out procedure, create a sign-out sheet with each camper's name listed to a row of blanks, one blank for each day for a parent/guardian to sign at dismissal time.

Employment or Internship Application

You may choose to recruit your own staff and thereby avoid the need to recruit or interview workers. However, if you do need to interview staff, you may need to obtain some typical application information. This is especially vital if you choose to use interns, as you will want to ensure you select the most highly qualified and professional interns. An application template is available at www.granadamusic.org, or you may choose to create your own document. Generally, an application includes:

- Demographics: General name and contact information section
- Employment history: Current and most recent place(s) of employment and position(s) held
- Education: Current and previous institutions and degrees earned
- Criminal record: The application should directly ask if the applicant has been arrested or convicted of a felony crime, and provide a space to describe the incident.
- References: Three to five professional references that can attest to the applicant's musicianship and suitability for working with children.
- Application questions: Include some basic questions to determine the applicant's motives, future goals, and other qualifications. Sample questions include:
- Describe why you want to work/intern at Camp Granada (what you want to learn or accomplish).
- Prior experiences working with children, either in musical or nonmusical activities
- Describe your career goals (for interns).

- List the musical and nonmusical activities, clubs, or organizations in which you currently participate (for interns).
- Signature line: The signature line should include a statement acknowledging that the information provided on the application is accurate to the best of the applicant's knowledge, and that misrepresentation on the application may lead to termination of employment.

Completion Certificate

If you choose to use interns in your program, you may need some type of letter or certificate of completion for the interns to submit to their sponsors or associations for completion of volunteer hours. Be sure the letter includes program name, dates, location, volunteer's name, number of hours completed, basic description of duties or job title, and your signature as the program director.

Incident Report Form

Parents appreciate regular and consistent communication, particularly regarding behavioral issues and medical concerns. If your host facility does not already have a "boo-boo report" or some other system of documentation, consider using an incident report form to document significant medical or behavioral issues that occurred throughout the day. A downloadable incident report form is available at www.granadamusic.org. The form should include:

- First and last name of child
- Date
- Nature of incident (behavioral/medical illness/other)
- Description: A blank space for staff to describe what happened
- Action taken: A blank space for staff to describe what steps were taken prior to the incident report form
- Signature lines for the staff member who completed the form, and for the program director

Closing Ceremony Program

Making a program for your closing ceremony is a nonessential, but highly recommended suggestion. In addition to listing performance selections, the program can be an excellent venue to promote upcoming events and general announcements (including your next session of Camp Granada), special recognition for those who contributed to your program, and something for campers to add to their scrapbooks, refrigerator doors, or other keepsake collections.

A program template for each theme is available at www.granadamusic.org, and general program suggestions are described below.

Cover Page

The cover page should include the Camp Granada main logo and theme logo (available at www.granadamusic.org), and the day, time, and location of your closing ceremony. You may also wish to include the name of your session director and/or other responsible persons.

Concert Etiquette Reminders

Expectations for concert etiquette differ from place to place, and your host organization may already have established protocol for concerts and events. General suggestions include:

- Please silence your cell phones and other communication devices.
- Babies and young children who need a break during the performance may be taken to the lobby.
- Food and drink are not permitted in the performance hall.

Performance Selections

The main function of the program is to list your performance selections in order. This allows parents to prepare their recording devices for the selections where their child may be featured, and lets them know what to expect. A program order for each theme is included in the introduction to the Curriculum Guide.

Introduction of Camp Staff

Provide a list of your camp staff, including volunteers, leaders, interns, and other workers who may have completed behind-the-scene tasks. It is best to list first and last name, along with a job title, or brief "special thanks" statements.

SPECIAL RECOGNITIONS

If your camp obtained donations of any kind (monetary donations, supplies, or parents who donated their time to help prepare for camp), it is a wise gesture to list names of each volunteer, sponsor, organization, or donor on the program.

Jeffrey Hardy Awards

The Jeffrey Hardy Award is given to campers who are aging-out of your program and who have attended three or more years of camp. As a gesture to these campers, list their names and the number of years they have attended camp on your closing ceremony program. In your first few years of camp, you may not have campers who fit the 3-year rule, so feel free to alter these criteria to best suit your program.

Dismissal Statement

To facilitate an easy dismissal time, provide a brief statement about how campers will be dismissed after the closing ceremony. Generally, parents need to know where to go to sign out their children after the closing ceremony, and a reminder about retrieving lunch boxes, art projects, and other personal belongings before leaving.

Join Us Next Year

Promote your next year's Camp Granada program with a reminder or note saying "Don't forget to join us next year." If possible, provide tentative dates for your next year's program.

Staff Shirts

Staff shirts contribute significantly to the professional image of your program. If you have the means to do so, and if you anticipate that your program will be successful (two or more years), embroider the Camp Granada logo (available www.granadamusic.org) on polo-style shirts for camp staff. If this is not possible, provide a free camp T-shirt for staff to wear on opening and closing day.

Scoreboard

To visually keep track of team scores, make a scoreboard to display in base camp or the cafeteria. The size of the scoreboard varies based on the size of your facilities. The general design of the scoreboard should include a row for each team, and a column for each day of camp plus one column for the cumulative score.

Team Flags

Team flags are optional decorations that generate a sense of team spirit throughout the week. They may also be used as a back drop during the closing ceremony. Camp Granada team colors are traditional red, blue, yellow, and green. Flags are traditionally made of broad cloth, and measure 30" wide by 24" high. You will also need a flagpole for each flag (wood dowels or curtain rods work well as flagpoles), and a stand or a base for each flagpole. For a lower-budget alternative, use colored, plastic table cloths to decorate lunch tables or other areas of your facilities.

Team Prize

The prize for the winning team is usually some sort of dessert or treat given at the end of the closing ceremony to celebrate the end of camp. Returning to the idea of team competition, the concern for winning and losing should never trump musical development at Camp Granada. Therefore, consider a way for every child to participate in the end-of-week party and for all campers to receive a prize of some kind, but continue to make it special for the team with the most points at the end of the week. For example, all campers receive the winning prize but the winning team gets to line up first.

A simple recipe that fits a camp theme is S'mores Snack Bowls. Ingredients include mini marshmallows (about ½ cup), chocolate chips (about 1 tablespoon), Teddy Grahams or Golden Grahams cereal (about ½ cup), and one waffle-cone bowl per camper. Divide Teddy Grahams and marshmallows into enough waffle-cone bowls for each camper. Heat chocolate chips until it melts. Drizzle over bowls to lightly coat the ingredients. Let cool, then serve.

Camp Traditions

Every successful camp has its traditions that children remember throughout their lives. Although camp traditions are not vital to the success of the program, they do contribute to the camp-like atmosphere of your program and generate a sense of authenticity for all who participate. Therefore, consider some fun, not-terribly-distracting traditions to implement in your program. Some suggestions are listed below.

Cecil (Camp Mascot)

Obtain a small figurine or other comical character that can serve as your camp's mascot, and give your mascot an unusual name. Tell the campers that the mascot sneaks around all day looking for campers with good attitudes, character, sportsmanship, and respect. Each morning, praise a camper who was "caught" the previous day demonstrating one of these attributes. Award this camper's team a certain number of points and allow the mascot to sit on that team's lunch table for the day.

Silly Rules and Procedures

Implement some silly rules to enforce (only if and when it will not interfere with learning or cause disruptive behaviors during instructional times). Some examples include all campers must say "cheezewhiz" whenever a leader sneezes; try to be the first person to touch your head whenever someone starts singing a song by (pick a famous singer).

Silly Songs

The "Order of the Fork" and "Where is Suzie?" are traditional camp songs and games that may be played during lunch or other downtimes, and will quickly become anticipated traditions of your program. The music for these songs is included below.

The Jeffrey Hardy Award

In the "Hello Muddah, Hello Faddah" song, Jeffry Hardy is the camper who goes missing. As your program grows, you will hopefully have campers who return from year to year. Over time, however, these campers will age out of the program and will no longer be eligible to return. The Jeffrey Hardy Award is a special recognition for campers who have attended two to three or more years of camp, and who are aging out of the program. You can choose to have a special certificate or plaque made for these campers, or create your own award for your program. The idea is to encourage campers to return from year to year, and thereby grow your program.

Chapter 2

Camp Songs

The materials in this section are for use during the Opening and Closing Sessions, during transitions, or whenever you have down time that can be filled with instructional fun.

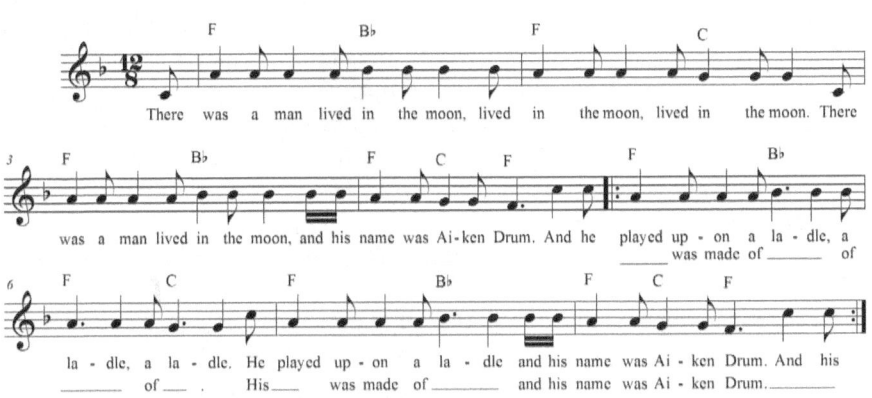

Figure 2.1 Aiken Drum. *Source*: Author

This is a Scottish folk song where children get to help write the lyrics. Each time you repeat the refrain, ask children to name an item of clothing that Aiken Drum is wearing, and name an item of food that the clothing is made from. For example, *his hat was made of pizza*. Repeat the song several times until Aiken Drum is fully dressed.

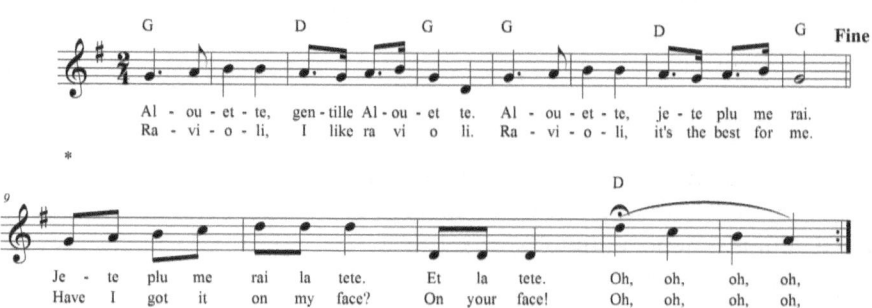

Figure 2.2 Alouette-Ravioli. *Source*: Author

This song is a cumulative song, getting longer each time it is repeated. The traditional French-Canadian, "Alouette," is a pretend song to sing to a bird you are preparing to cook. Loosely translated, it means. "Bird, gentle bird. I am going to pluck your feathers out. The feathers from your head (tete), your beak (bek), …" Each time you repeat this song, add another body part as you sing the octaves. Then hold the "oh" fermata, and repeat.

First time: Jete plumerai la tete (high), Et la tete (low)
Second time: Jete plumerai le bec (high), et le bec (low); e la tete (high), et la tete (low)
Third time: Jete plumerai le cou (high), et le cou (low); et le bec (high), et le bec (low); et la tete (high), et la tete (low)
Continue adding a body part each time. Body parts and translations include:

- la tete (head)
- le bek (beak)
- le cou (neck)
- lex yeux (eyes)
- les ailes (wings)
- les pattes (legs)

- la queue (tail)
- le dos (back)

When singing the Ravioli adaptation, use the same form as "Alouette," adding an additional body part or item with each repetition, and repeat once high, and once low:

First time: Have I got it on my face (high), on my face (low)?
Second time: Have I got it on my shirt (high), on my shirt (low)? On my face (high), on my face (low)?
Continue until the end.

"BABY SHARK"

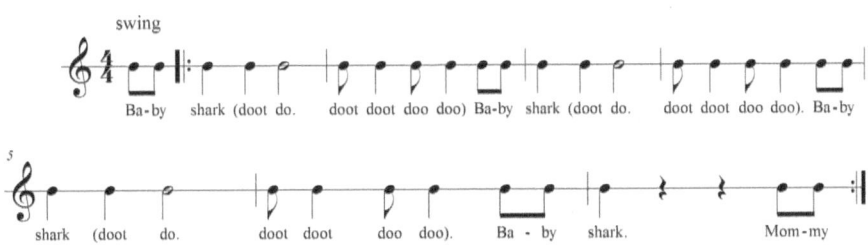

Figure 2.3 Baby Shark. *Source*: Author

Repeat several times using these words and motions:

Baby shark:	Pointer fingers and thumbs moving like small mouths
Mommy shark:	Both hands moving like larger mouths
Daddy shark:	Both arms working as one giant mouth, fingers like teeth
Grampa shark:	Both arms working as one giant mouth, fingers in (no teeth)
Going swimming:	Pretend to swim
Here they come:	Make your two hands look like shark fins poking out of the water
Swimming faster:	Pretend to swim very fast
Shark attack:	Make hands go up and down
Lost my arm:	Pretend to swim with one arm
Lost my leg:	Swim with one arm, standing on one leg
Lost my head:	Swim with one arm, standing on one leg, holding head down
CPR:	Pretend to do CPR
It's too late:	Pretend to cry

"BOOM CHICK-A-BOOM"

Scout Song

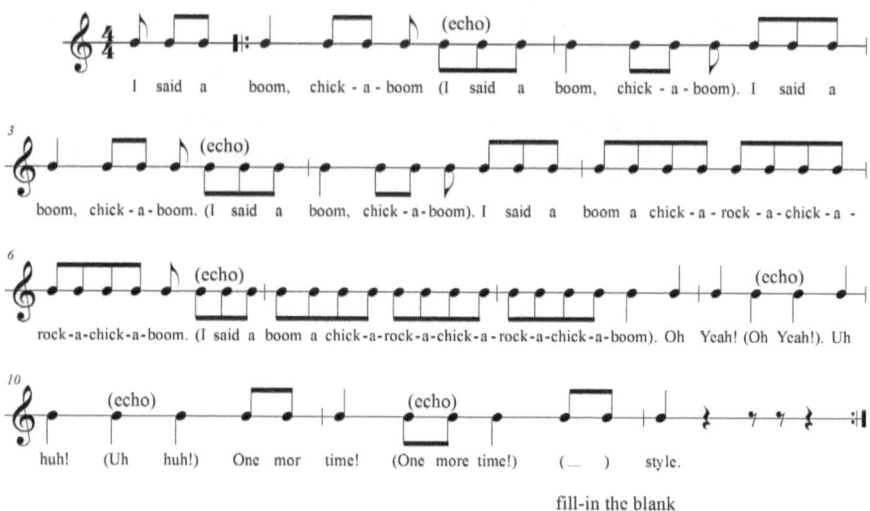

Figure 2.4 **Boom Chick-a-Boom.** *Source*: Author

Additional Lyrics

Janitor Style (hold a pretend broom and sweep back and forth to the beat)
I said a Broom Sweep-a Broom; (repeat); I said a Broom Sweep-a Mop-a Sweep-a Mop-a Sweep-a BroomValley Girl Style (move pretend pom-poms up and down to the beat)
I said like boom chick-a-boom; (repeat); I said like boom chick-a like rocka chick whatever chick-a-boom.
Baby Style: normal lyrics, spoken with a high voice
Football Style: normal lyrics, spoken with deep, grunting voice.
Allow campers to make up new styles with suitable voices, and motions. Or, additional lyrics and motions are available on numerous camp song and scouting websites.

"THE BUTTON FACTORY"

Camp Song

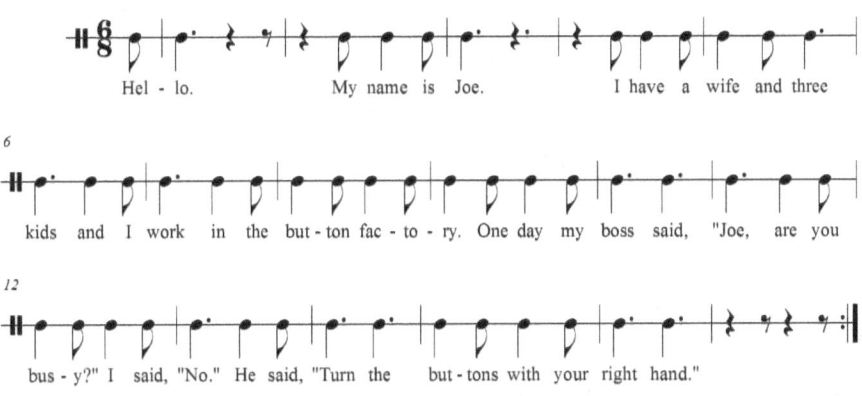

Figure 2.5 **Button Factory.** *Source*: Author

At the end, pretend to turn a large button to the beat, then repeat. At the end of the second time, turn the buttons with the left hand and add the left hand to the movement. With each additional repetition, add a body part and motion:

- Right foot
- Left foot
- Head
- Tongue (stick out your tongue and say the poem one last time with all movements)

When the boss asks if you're busy, this time say "YES!!"

"CHE CHE KOOLAY"

Ghana folk song

Figure 2.6 Che Che Koolay. *Source*: Author

As you lead the campers in "Che Che Koolay," improvise motions as you sing, and invite campers to echo with voices and movement.

"CLAP YOUR HANDS"

Traditional

Figure 2.7 Clap Your Hands. *Source*: Author

Repeat this song several times, creating new movements: Stomp your feet, nod your head, pat your legs, others. Also, invite campers to create new words and movements. On the refrain ("li, li, li"), raise your hands above your head and turn in a circle.

"FOUND A PEANUT"

(tune of Oh My Darling)

Traditional Song and Adaptation

Figure 2.8 Found a Peanut. *Source*: Author

Repeat the melody several times, inviting campers to create new verses that tell a story about what they do with their peanut and what happens to them.

"FRIED HAM"

Camp Song

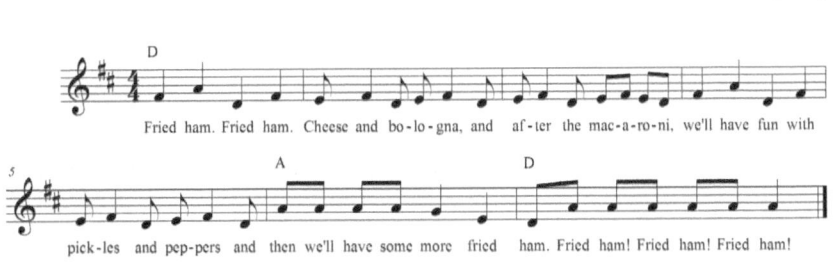

Figure 2.9 Fried Ham. *Source*: Author

After each verse, say "Same song, second verse. _____ accent. A whole lot worse." Fill in the blank with types of accents, and then repeat the song, singing in the appropriate style. Examples:

Football accent (sing with a deep, military-sounding voice)
Cowboy accent (sing with a twangy drawl)
Opera accent (sing with a big, boistrous voice)
Chipmunk accent (double tempo, up the octave)

"THE GREEN GRASS GROWS ALL AROUND"

Children's Song

Figure 2.10 The Green Grass Grows All Around. *Source*: Author

Verse 2: And on that tree, there was a branch. The prettiest branch that you ever did see …

*At this point, the song gets longer each time it is repeated

Verse 2, add: And the branch on the tree, and the tree in the hole, and the hole in the ground …

Verse 3: And on that branch there was a leaf

Verse 4: And on that leaf, there was a nest

Verse 5: And in that nest, there was an egg

Verse 6: And in that egg there was a bird

Verse 7: And on that bird there was a wing

(continue as you wish: feather, bug, etc.)

"HEY, BURRITO!"

Figure 2.11 Hey, Burrito. *Source*: Author

"I LOVE THE MOUNTAINS"

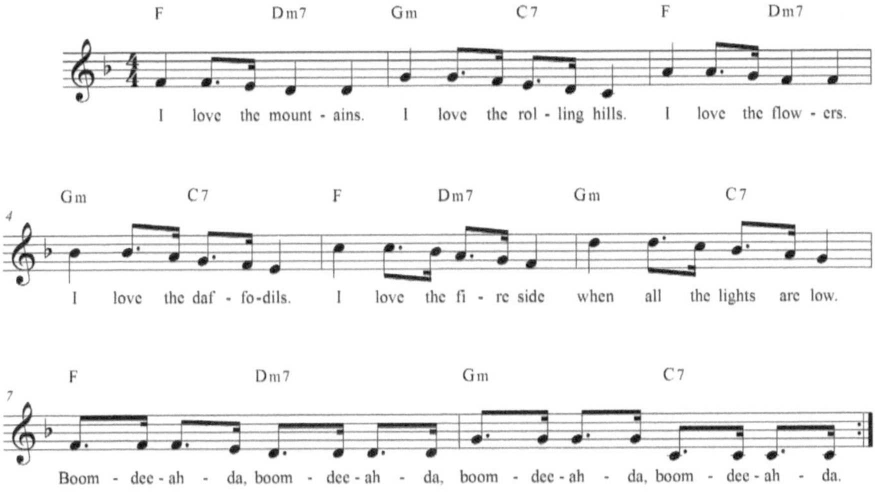

Figure 2.12 I Love the Mountains. *Source*: Author

"IF ALL OF THE RAINDROPS"

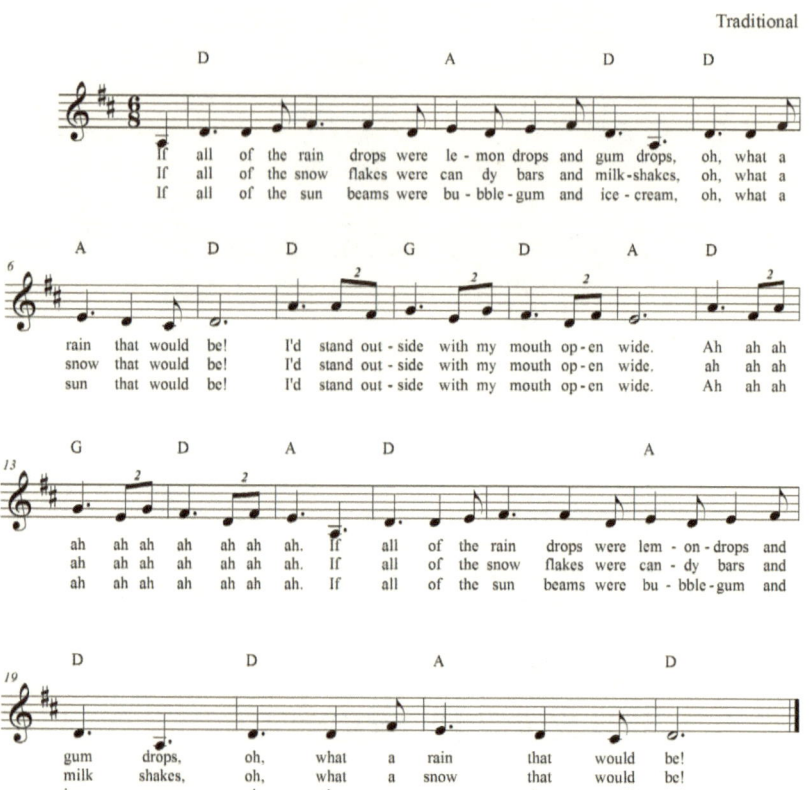

Figure 2.13 If All of the Raindrops. *Source*: Author

"I MET A BEAR"

Figure 2.14 I Met a Bear. *Source*: Author

Additional verses (echo after each line, then sing all lines together)
He looked at me, I looked at him. He sized up me, I sized up him.
He said to me, "Why don't you run? I see you don't have any gun."
And so I ran, away from there. But right behind me, was that bear.
In front of me, there was a tree. A great big tree, oh, glory be!
The lowest branch, was ten feet up. I thought I'd jump, and trust my luck.
And so I jumped, into the air. But I missed that branch, oh, way up there.
Now don't you fret, and don't you frown. I caught that branch, on the way back down!
This is the end. There is no more, unless I see, that bear once more.

"MY BONNIE LIES OVER THE OCEAN"

Traditional (Scotland)

Figure 2.15 My Bonnie Lies over the Ocean. *Source*: Author

As you sing this song, stand up or sit down each time you sing a word that starts with B.

"OH, MY AUNT CAME BACK"

Traditional

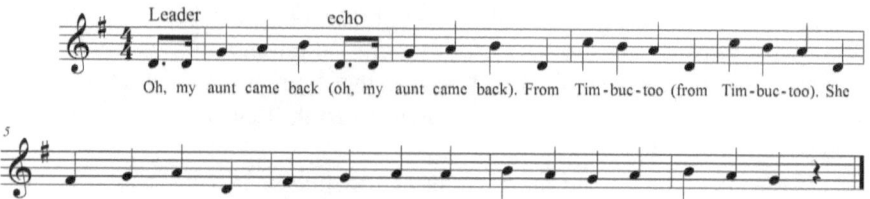

Figure 2.16 **Oh, My Aunt Came Back.** *Source*: Author

Additional Lyrics and Movements

Oh, my aunt came back from old Japan, and she brought with her a waving fan (wave with one hand)

Oh, my aunt came back from old Algiers, and she brought with her a pair of shears (scissors motion with other hand)

Oh, my aunt came back from the country fair, and she brought with her a rocking chair (rock back and forth)

Oh, my aunt came back from Guadalupe, and she brought with her a Hula Hoop (swing hips)

Oh, my aunt came back from Niagara Falls, and she brought with her some ping pong balls (move head back and forth)

Oh, my aunt came back from the city zoo, and she brought with her a nut like you.

"OLD LADY LEARY"

Traditional

Figure 2.17 **Old Lady Leary.** *Source*: Author

This is a song about the Great Chicago fire of 1881. It was rumored that Old Lady Leary left a lantern in her barn at night and, "when the cow kicked it over," it ignited the barn, and the fire spread until most of the city of Chicago was in ashes.

Repeat the song six times. The first time, sing all words. The second time, remove the word "bed" and clap in its place (Late last night, when we were all in [clap]). Each time the song is repeated, remove the next underlined word and clap in its place. Continue until all underlined words are removed.

Figure 2.18 Old Woman All Skin and Bones. *Source*: Author

"THE ORDER OF THE FORK"

Figure 2.19 The Order of the Fork. *Source*: Author

"The Order of the Fork" is a traditional camp song/game played during meals. On random days, a small group of camp staff or campers form a line outside the dining area and march into the room singing "The Order of the Fork," each holding up a plastic fork. At the end of the song, the line stops behind camper to be initiated.

The group proclaims in unison, "Stand up please (wait). Bend over please (wait). 2—4—6—8— we initiate you! Uh! (pretend to poke camper in rear end)." The new member gets a fork and joins at the end of the line, and the singing and parade begins again.

Camp Songs

"RAM SAM SAM"

Folk song from Morocco

Figure 2.20 Ram Sam Sam. *Source*: Author

"A SAILOR WENT TO SEA"

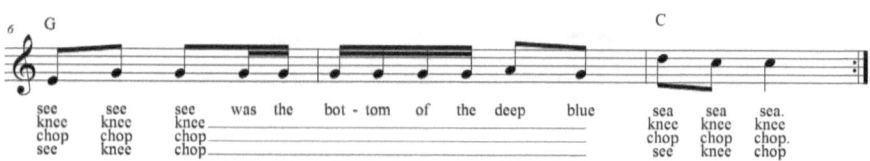

Figure 2.21 A Sailor Went to Sea. *Source*: Author

"SING WHEN THE SPRIT SAYS SING"

Figure 2.22 Sing When the Sprit Says Sing. *Source*: Author

Other Verses:
You gotta clap ... (clap on beats one and three)
You gotta hum ...
You gotta snap ... (snap on beats two and four)
You gotta stomp ... (stomp on beats one and three while singing loudly)
You gotta hush ... (singing quietly)
You gotta sing ... (sing normally)

"SINGING IN THE RAIN"

Camp Adaptation

Figure 2.23 Singing in the Rain. *Source*: Author

Motions: On the high-hat part, wave hands back and forth like windshield wipers
  At the end:

Leader: (spoken) Thumbs out! (stick thumbs out)—group echos

Repeat entire song.

Leader: Thumbs out (echo) Elbows back (echo) Repeat entire song.

Next: Thumbs out (echo) elbows back (echo) Knees bent (echo)

Next: Thumbs out (echo) elbows back (echo) Knees bent (echo) Knees together (echo)

Keep adding one movement at the end each time: Booty out, head back, tongue out.

"THERE'S A HOLE AT THE BOTTOM OF THE SEA"

Children's Song

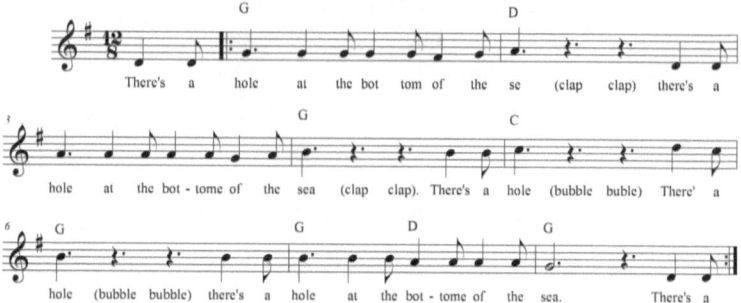

Figure 2.24 There's a Hole at the Bottom of the Sea. *Source*: Author

Repeat multiple times—each time making the song longer:

Verse 2: There's a log in the hole at the bottom of the sea (clap clap)

Verse 3: There's a bump on the log in the hole at the bottom of the sea (clap clap)

Verse 4: There's a frog on the bump on the log in the hole at the bottom of the sea (clap clap)

Verse 5: There's a fly on the frog on the bump on the log in the hole at the bottom of the sea (clap clap)

Verse 6: There's a wing on the fly on the frog on the bump on the log in the hole at the bottom of the sea (clap clap)

Verse 7: There's a flea on the wing, on the fly ...

"WADDALY ATCHA"

Perform "Waddaly Atcha" with a hand jive to the steady beat (each line represents one measure):

Pat pat clap clap

wave left hand over right (2 times) wave right hand over left (2 times)

right hand touch nose then left shoulder left hand touch nose then right shoulder

right hand wave twice left hand wave twice

Repeat

On the last "whoo"—raise both hands in the air

Scout song

Figure 2.25 Waddaly Atcha. *Source*: Author

Additional Lyrics

Please sing to me that sweet melody called doodley doo, doodley doo.
I like the rest, but the part I like best Goes doodley doo, doodley doo.
It's the simplest thing there isn't much to it
I like it so, wherever I go, It's doodley doodley doo.

"WHERE IS SUZIE?"

Suzie is an old camp game based on the song "Paw Paw Patch" (Where, oh Where is Suzie?). Pick a day or two to teach Suzie to the campers and play the accompanying game. For this game, you will need a wooden nickel (available at most craft shops) and decorate it with a cartoon drawing of a girl, or a simple letter "S" for Suzie.

At the beginning of the day, the camp director (or designee) will sneak Suzie into the pocket or other place of one of the campers or leaders. During the opening session, the singing of the Suzie song will signify that Suzie has been hidden. Throughout the day, the person with Suzie is to try to sneak Suzie onto someone else. At lunch or in the coda session at the end of the day, the Suzie song will be sung again, signifying that the game is over and the person with Suzie must do something embarrassing or silly for the group.

Figure 2.26 Where is Suzie. *Source*: Author

General Rules

You cannot put Suzie in a place that will embarrass someone. You cannot put Suzie in a bag or lunch box. It must be placed on the person. If the person feels you trying to give them Suzie, you must take it back and try again with someone else.

General Strategy

If you find that someone snuck Suzie onto you, keep it a secret, otherwise people will avoid you all day, and you will be stuck with her.

Part 2

CURRICULUM GUIDE

CURRICULUM OVERVIEW

The **Spaced Out!** theme takes students on a musical journey through outer space, studying the music of Gustav Holst, and folk songs from around the world. The lessons teach campers and parents about the Voyager satellites launched in 1970, each containing a gold disk with songs and pictures from Earth to teach beings on other planets what life is like on Earth.

The closing ceremony includes a parody of a 1938 radio broadcast that made listeners believe the world was being invaded by space aliens. In truth, the broadcast was the radio station's Halloween prank: a dramatic reading of Orson Wells' "War of the Worlds." For the Camp Granada closing ceremony, the premise is that the golden recorders on Voyager reached Pluto where life forms liked the music so much that they wanted to come to earth to hear some more.

Younger campers will perform an English folk story, "The Strange Visitor," adding sound effects with voices and instruments, and will perform "Sally Go Round the Sun" with movement and non-pitched percussion. The middle group will perform a rhythm-stick and body-percussion accompaniment of "Funga Alafia," a Nigerian greeting song (to welcome our visitors from Pluto), and will use boomwhackers to accompany "Aiken Drum."

The older campers will perform a French folk song, "Au Clair de la Lune" (by moonlight) on recorders and pitched percussion, "The Car Song" using nontraditional instruments to sound like a ratty spaceship about to fall apart, and will compose an improvisation piece using pitched percussion as a song for Pluto. All campers will also sing "Sorida," a welcome song from Zimbabwe, and our Camp Granada theme song, "Hello Muddah, Hello Faddah."

In Connections class, younger campers will make a satellite kazoo from a recycled toilet-paper tube, and a UFO ocean drum from paper plates. Older campers will create a self-portrait as if they are floating away in space. All campers will create a craft project to learn about Gustav Holst's *The Planets*, design their own alien in the style of African masks, and will make their own solar system in the style of Eric Carle.

At the time this curriculum was written, there were many conveniently timed connections between the **Spaced Out!** theme and science. As a few examples, Pluto was categorized again as a dwarf planet after a few years of being declassified as a planet; the Voyager probes reached Pluto approximately the same week of camp; and a solar eclipse occurred within months of camp. As you plan for your own **Spaced Out!** camp session, browse your local news station to see what astronomical or scientific innovations are underway.

CLOSING CEREMONY ADMINISTRATIVE PREPARATION

The Program

The closing ceremony for the *Spaced Out!* theme is unlike any other Camp Granada theme. The main difference is that the other themes conclude with a regular recital format where there is no real script other than a list of performance selections. The *Spaced Out!* theme, however, includes a script (later in this book) with lines for staff or interns, and the performance selections are imbedded in the script.

SPACED OUT! FONTS

There are two specific fonts used in the *Spaced Out!* Theme. The font for the main logo is Space Age, available for free download from www.dafont.com/space-age.font. The other font, used for additional theme-based memos and general lettering, is Moon House, available for free download from www.dafont.com/moonhouse.font.

GUEST ALIEN

The closing ceremony for *Spaced Out!* theme calls for a guest speaker or, more precisely a "guest alien." Well in advance of your closing day, invite a guest speaker to play the part of the alien, and provide some basic information your guest will need to know (when to report, what to say, etc.). Most of this information is described in the script. The guest alien can be a local celebrity who supports music education, a principal, administrator, or someone else of significance that supports music in your local community.

PROGRAM ORDER

"Sorida," Zimbabwe folk song
"Au Clair de la Lune" (Moonlight), French folk song
"Hello Muddah, Hello Faddah" (maybe)
"Aiken Drum," Scottish folk song
"The Strange Visitor," English folk tale
"Hello Muddah, Hello Faddah" (we hope)
"The Car Song," traditional children's song
"Sally Go Round the Sun," traditional children's song
"Hello Muddah, Hello Faddah" (possibly)

"Funga Alafia," Nigerian welcome song
"A Song for Pluto," written by the campers
Introduction of Camp Staff
Jeffrey Hardy Awards
"Hello Muddah, Hello Faddah," music by Lou Busch; lyrics by Alan Sherman
Announcement of Final Points and Dismissal Party

CLOSING CEREMONY SCRIPT

Overview

The script for this theme's closing ceremony is a parody of a 1938 radio broadcast that made listeners believe the world was being invaded by space aliens. The performance is staged like a regular closing ceremony or performance, but is periodically interrupted by news anchors who are tracking a developing story of an alien spaceship that takes off from the planet Pluto and crash-lands on Earth, very close to Camp Granada. For the best effect, begin the closing ceremony as if nothing unusual is going on and act as though the interruptions are genuine (although it will be clear that they are not). Also for best effect, do not tell the campers about the alien surprise visitor at the end of the script).

MUSICAL SELECTIONS

For this program, all campers will learn to sing all of the musical selections. Different age groups will accompany the singing with age-appropriate arrangements using pitched and non-pitched percussion, recorders, and novelty instruments.

CHARACTERS

News Anchor

Can be camp staff or campers. The script is written for one news anchor. If you wish to use more, divide the script into a suitable number of parts.

Field Reporter

Can be camp staff or campers.
Camera Crew (optional/silent role)

Camp staff or camper to hold the camera.
Camp Director
As him/herself to coordinate the performance.
Alien Guest

Alien(s) who have arrived from the planet Pluto. Well in advance of the camp session, invite a person or persons of significance who will be willing to serve as your guest alien. The purpose of this is for a bit of humor for the campers so the person you pick should be familiar to the campers (the campers will find it funny that this person is actually an alien). The purpose of this is also to advocate for your program in the community so the guest alien should be someone of significance (your campus principal, district administrator, or local celebrity who supports the arts). An optional line in the script provides time for the guest alien to directly address the audience, if he/she desires. This is a time for the guest, speaking as him or herself, to address the audience, advocate for the arts and/or for your music program, and thanking the audience for supporting the arts in the community.

STAGING AND SET NEEDS

Set the stage with the main performance area in the center. You will need an area for the children to stand/sit while they are singing, and an additional area for instrumental performances. Off to one side, you will need a separate area to set a news anchor desk. This can be as simple as a fold-up table or a student desk, or as elaborate as your imagination can create.

Campers/staff at the news desk can have copies of the script to avoid the need for memorization. In large performance spaces, speakers will need to have microphones. Nonfunctioning microphones may also be used as props for the news anchors. If you have the available technology, set up a smartboard, TV monitor, or projection screen behind the news anchor desk for the video feed from the camera (see *Optional technology needs* below).

The field reporter and camera crew need to set up offstage but with easy access to the stage area. For this staging to work, you will need a video camera and a way to project the camera's live image on the screen behind the news anchor. This should appear as though the field reporter is actually on location. If technology is unavailable to have the field reporter offstage, set up the reporter on the opposite side of the stage from the news anchor desk, with the campers in center stage.

Regarding instruments, you will need all equipment and instruments for the campers to perform the songs included in the Spaced Out curriculum. Prior to the start of the program, set out all the instruments for each song in the program. As each group performs their songs and instruments are no longer needed, campers may remove instruments from the stage as they transition from the instrument sections of the stage to the risers. Additional blocking and staging transitions are described throughout the script.

LIGHTING NEEDS (OPTIONAL)

If lighting is available, program three lighting scenes: One should light the news anchor desk (stage right); one should light the main performance area (singing and instruments—center stage); and one should light the roving reporter (stage left) if technology is not available to have this person backstage.

TECHNOLOGY NEEDS

High Priority

For the best effect, obtain an audio file of the type of music that a special news bulletin might use to interrupt a television program (there are multiple examples online available for free download).

Medium Priority

If your performance space regularly uses sound amplification, you will need microphones for the news anchors, field reporter, and for the director.

Low Priority

Obtain a recording of *Colonel Bogeys March* or other suitable example to play over loud speakers as campers march into place to begin the performance.

SCENE ONE

The play opens as a regular closing ceremony. Stage left/right lights are dimmed so the audience can only see the main performance area (center stage). Play *Colonel Bogeys March* over the sound system for campers to march onto the stage and get into position.

Tech: *Lights up on center stage (campers) only.*

Director: (to audience) Good afternoon ladies and gentlemen. Thank you very much for coming to today's closing ceremony at Camp Granada. Although we spent our week learning about space, we would like to begin the program with a song from right here on planet earth. This is a traditional welcome song from Zimbabwe called *Sorida*.

SONG: "Sorida"

Director: (to audience) Thank you very much. Moving right along, we would like to perform for you our camp's namesake song called "Hello Muddah, Hello Faddah." This song is a story about a camper who is writing a letter home to mom and dad. Let's hear what this camper had to say. *Get set to lead campers in the Hello Muddah Song.*

Tech: *Accompanist should begin playing the introduction to 'Hello Muddah, Hello Faddah.' Just before the singers begin, the performance should be interrupted by the recording of the news music, played over loud speakers.*

Director and campers: *Look around as if confused about what is going on.*

Tech: *Fade out center-stage lights as news anchor begins to talk.*

News anchor: We interrupt this program for a special news bulletin. We apologize for interrupting the Camp Granada closing ceremonies and we will take you back to that program just as soon as possible. We're covering a developing story as events unfold and we want to keep you up-to-date with the latest information.

According to NASA, in July of 2015, the Voyager satellite reached the orbit of Pluto, the last and smallest planet in our solar system. Some of you may recall that the Voyager probes were launched by NASA in 1970 in search of life on other planets, and each probe contained a gold disk with pictures and music from Earth. Scientists at the time believed that if there is, indeed, life on other planets, these gold records would help them learn about life on Earth.

Moments ago, NASA scientists recorded video footage from Voyager of a large blast from Pluto's surface, and what appeared to be a meteor headed straight for the Voyager shuttle. As the object came closer to Voyager, cameras identified the object as some sort of spacecraft launched from the planet's surface. As you can imagine, this footage is history in the making as we now have confirmed, visual evidence of life on other planets.

Although this is amazing, this is not the first evidence of alien life forms. Just after the blast from Pluto's surface was recorded, chief NASA officers met with the president who immediately held a press conference and released a NASA file that, until today, has been classified. This file contains letters from Apollo 17 astronaut Eugene Cernan, the last American to walk on the moon, and his description of an encounter with a "moon man" by the name of Aiken Drum. Astronaut Cernan's report described him this way.

Tech: *Fade in center stage lights/fade out news desk lights.*

SONG: "Aiken Drum"

Tech: *Fade out center-stage lights/fade in news desk lights.*

News anchor: *(speaking to campers in response to Aiken Drum)* Well that's just silly *(back to audience/camera)* In addition to the Aiken Drum sighting, there has been one other documented visit from a being from another world. An English fairy tale tells the story of an old lady and her strange visitor. We have uncovered video footage of this story that, until recently, was also classified. We should warn you that young children may find this story alarming.

Tech: *Fade in center-stage lights/fade out news desk lights.*

SONG: "The Strange Visitor"

Tech: *Fade out center-stage lights/fade in news desk lights.*

News anchor: *(before lights fade up on the news desk, get into a hiding position behind the news desk, as though you're afraid of the visitor, peering from under the desk. When you realize the lights are back on the news desk, awkwardly get back into your chair as though you're embarrassed about being afraid).* Sorry about that. I....uh..... was tying my shoe.... Yeah.....that's it...... We take you back now to the Camp Granada closing ceremony in ____ (city) currently underway but will remain at the news desk and will share what we can about this strange event from the planet Pluto as this story unfolds.

Tech: *(lights dim on news desk/lights up on campers)*

Director: *(sitting center stage in front of the campers, reading a book—begin speaking to pretend someone offstage)* Are we back? Are we on? *(now address audience).* I'm sorry about that ladies and gentlemen. You came to hear your children perform so without further ado, we give you *Hello Muddah, Hello Faddah.*

Tech: Play the introduction to 'Hello Muddah, Hello Faddah' again, and interrupt with news music just before singers begin verse one.

Director and campers: I don't believe this! Again!? (ad lib...etc.)

News anchor: Parents and family members, I'm sorry to interrupt the closing ceremony again but we have more breaking news to bring to you. NASA spokespeople have just released this statement and have asked news stations across the country to share with you.

People of America. NASA scientists have been tracking unusual activity on the surface of the planet Pluto and what appears to be a spacecraft, launched from Pluto's surface, heading very quickly in a direct path toward earth.

Over the past few hours, we have made two attempts to intercept the craft and can now tell you that both attempts have failed. With our current technology, the only way to get astronauts back into space is to use one of the space shuttles. But, since the space shuttle program was deactivated, most of the shuttles were donated to museums and we have no other crafts suitable for deep space flight. Early this morning, shuttle mechanics were sent to the museums to get the ships back into working order. One mechanic, working on the space shuttle Atlantis at the Kennedy Space Center, tried to start the ship's engine and recorded this unusual sound from the engine compartment.

Tech: *Fade in center-stage lights/fade out news desk lights.*

SONG: "The Car Song"

Tech: *Fade out center-stage lights/fade in news desk lights.*

News anchor: Initial analysis revealed that the ship's engine had been removed and replaced by a bunch of small percussion instruments. Once the instruments were removed and the engine replaced, a test flight revealed an additional problem with the ship's navigation system. When the Shuttles were sent to the museums, their original navigation computers were removed and replaced with a newer system build by the Space Administration Location Lynk, or SALLY corporation. It turns out that SALLY's computer system will only make left turns, sending the shuttles in circles whenever they are launched. During its test flight, NASA analysts were able to make this recording of the ship's navigational computer:

Tech: *Fade in center-stage lights/fade out news desk lights.*

SONG: "Sally Go Round the Sun"

Tech: *Fade out center-stage lights/fade in news desk lights.*

News anchor: (*still reading the letter from NASA*) So now, in addition to a UFO hurling toward planet Earth, our entire fleet of space shuttles is spinning though space in an endless left turn—like NASCAR with wings. And so, we regret to inform you that we have no other way to intercept the alien spacecraft heading toward earth, and until the ship gets closer, we have no way of communicating with the alien craft. We will send additional information as it becomes available.

(*directing attention to audience*) So ladies and gentlemen, we at channel six news are committed to standing by you as this situation unfolds and will bring you the most up-to-date information as it becomes available. In the meantime, we take you back to the Camp Granada closing ceremonies, still underway in _____ (city).

Tech: *Fade in center-stage lights; **keep lights on news desk up this time.*

Directors and campers: *Asleep on the risers, in chairs, etc. (some snoring).*

News anchor: (*emphatically—looking toward stage*) I said "We take you back to Camp Granada!!!!"

Directors and campers: (*still sleeping*)

News anchor: (*get up and walk to stage area. Hit a gong, or a drum to make a loud noise that will wake up the campers and staff. Walk back to news desk*)

Directors and campers: (*startled and jump up at the sound of the instrument*) Sorry! I'm awake. What happened? (ad lib, etc.) Ladies and gentlemen. Once again, we bring you *Hello Muddah, Hello Faddah*.... I hope.

Tech: *Begin the introduction to 'Hello Muddah, Hello Faddah' and interrupt it with the news music one last time. Here, interrupt the accompaniment a little earlier than before.*

Director and campers: (*very frustrated/throw hands in the air, sit down angrily, etc.*)

Really?!? Aw man! Can we just sing the song?! Etc.

News anchor: (*talking to campers and to audience, over the noise of the campers*) I'm really sorry, everybody. I just received this update. I'm only doing my job.

Director and campers: Yeah, yeah! Whatever, etc. ad lib.

News anchor: Well I am; and I do apologize again for the interruption. We've just received an update from our reporter in the field. It seems that the alien spacecraft from Pluto has in fact landed and our field reporter is live at the scene. (*talking into earpiece*). _____ (*name*)—can you hear us?

Field reporter: *Set up offstage, talking into a camera, with live feed showing on stage. If this technology is not available, have the field reporter set-up on stage, on the opposite side of the stage from the news desk, and face the audience as if looking into a camera.*

Tech (optional): *Bring-up camera image on the screen or lights on the field reporter.*

Field reporter: Yes, I can hear you and we're live at the landing site, just outside of the Camp Granada closing ceremonies. The alien craft landed just outside the _____ (*building*) and the creature was seen heading into the _____ (*room*). We're going inside now to see what we find.

Director: (*talking over the field reporter*) Wait—where are they?

Field reporter and camera crew: *Come onto the stage or to center stage to interact with director.*

Campers and camp staff: (*act confused. Some campers "wave to mom" on the camera, and do other typical "I'm on camera" antics*)

Field reporter: We're now live inside the _____ (*room*) at the closing ceremony of Camp Granada where witnesses say the alien was last seen. We're with the Camp Granada director live in _____ (*name of city or campus*). Tell me (*to director*), have you seen anything unusual this afternoon?

Director: Define "unusual"! We're just trying to hold our closing ceremony and sing some songs for the people in the audience!

Reporter: But witnesses have confirmed an alien sighting in your building...

Director: (*interrupting*) The only thing I've seen in this building today that isn't supposed to be here is you. So if you don't mind, we're trying to give a concert.... (*Interrupted by doorbell sound from back stage. Camper or staff member will play sol-mi on a metallophone to sound like a door bell. At this point, the guest aliens should be in place backstage, behind the door.*) **Director:** (*walking back stage to open door*) Now what? I didn't even know this place had a doorbell!

Field reporter: (*talking to camera—walking with director*) The director has not seen anything unusual, but someone has just rang the doorbell and we're going now to see who's at the door.

Director: (*Open door.*)

Field reporter (*Standing on stage, but talking to alien guest who is offstage [hidden from audience]—use the microphone as a reporter would to make sure the audience can hear the alien guest.*) Are you the pilot of the spaceship that just took-off from Pluto and landed on Earth?

Alien guest: I am.

Field reporter: Are you here to take over the planet?

Alien guest: No, I am not here to take over the planet.

Field reporter: Are you here to run for government office?

Alien guest: No, I am not. There are too many of us in office already.

Field reporter: The whole world is waiting to see you. Would you mind showing yourself to the audience?

Alien guest: Sure

(*Alien, director, and field reporter walk to center stage.*)

Field reporter: If I may say, you don't look too much like an alien. In fact, you look a lot like _____ (*name and title of guest alien*).

Alien guest: I am in disguise so I won't scare any of the children.

Field reporter: Is that so. Well if you're not here to take-over the planet, why are you here?

Alien guest: Several years ago, your planet launched this Voyager satellite thing that just made its way to Pluto. We brought it down to the planet to study it and, inside, we found this gold record with music and pictures from your planet. We really like the music and we wanted to hear some more, so we thought we would come to earth to see what we could find.

Director: *(interjecting into the conversation)* Hey! I've got an idea. This is a music camp and all day long, these campers have been trying to sing some songs, but for some reason *(glare at field reporter and news anchor)*, we have not been able to do too much. Would you like to hear some of our songs?

Alien guest: That would be wonderful. Can I go sit down out there *(pointing to audience)* to listen?

Director: You most certainly may.

(Optional) But before you do, do you have anything to say to the people of planet earth?

Optional time in program for guest to address the audience (alien guest goes to sit down/students & director get set to perform):

Field reporter: *(talking to camera)* We are witnessing history in what may be the first true interaction between humans and a being from another planet. A spaceship from Pluto has landed here in _____ (city) after beings from that planet intercepted the gold record from Voyager and requested to hear more earth music. The children here at Camp Granada are going to begin by welcoming the Plutonian with a traditional greeting song from Nigeria called *Funga Alafia*. We take you now to their live performance currently in progress. I am _____ (name), field reporter for channel six news. *(slip offstage as children perform)*

Tech: *Lights left and right fade/center-stage lights should still be up.*

SONG: "Funga Alafia"

NOTE: From this point forward, there is no real need for a script. The director needs only to introduce the next pieces on the program, and making closing remarks as needed.

Director: *(to audience)* The next piece is based on *Planets* by Gustav Holst. *Planets* is a collection of pieces based on the Greek mythological character for whom each planet was named. Holst wrote this piece between 1914 and 1915 but Pluto was not discovered until 1930 so Holst did not include a song for Pluto in his music.

This week, the campers composed a song for Pluto using some of the same techniques that Holst may have used when he composed the rest of the music back in 1914. Mainly, we copied Holst's idea of making the song sound like its character. The campers got to decide, not just the notes that would be played, but also how they would be performed—whether loud or soft, fast or slow, or other ways to perform the notes. In Greek mythology, Pluto was in charge of the underworld so we talked about dark caves, the creepy sounds you might hear, some of the critters you might see, and then tried to make our song sound like that experience.

Finally, this piece is written in the style of a tone row. In a tone row, the composer does not really try to write a recognizable or singable melody. Instead, the composer follows a set of guidelines or rules for how the notes in a scale can be used. Mainly, there are three basic rules: First, the melody has to use all of the notes in the scale. Second, the notes have to be used out of order. And, third, once a note is used, it cannot be used again until all of the notes in the scale have been performed at least once. For our song, we are using a five-note scale so we challenge you to try to recognize when all five pitches of the scale have been used.

We hope you enjoy an original composition, written and performed by the upper elementary class.

SONG: "Pluto"

Director: For those of you who have sent your children to Camp Granada in the past, you've probably realized that this year's closing ceremony was a bit different. In keeping with our space theme this year, our closing ceremony was a kid-friendly spoof of a real event that happened in 1938. A radio broadcast of a symphony orchestra concert was interrupted with what listeners believed to be a live news report of alien ships landing on earth and blowing up entire cities with their laser beams and death rays. It obviously turned out to be a hoax; it was the radio station's Halloween prank and what people thought was a news report was really a dramatic reading of Orson Wells' *War of the Worlds*.

We hope you enjoyed our rendition of this broadcast and would like to thank _____ (name) for being our guest alien today. *[Insert brief bit of information about alien guest and allow him/her to say a word about Camp Granada if possible.]* We would also like to take this time to introduce our camp staff who also participated in our broadcast.
[Introduce all camp staff and interns.]

We also have to announce our winning team and let you know what to do at the close of the concert. The boys and girls have been on teams all week, competing for points in games and activities, and they have waited all day to see the final points.

[Announce the prize you selected for your campers, and announce team results from fourth to first place.]

Also take a few minutes to discuss your program's dismissal procedure once the closing ceremony is finished. Parents need to know where to go to get their children, where to get their lunch boxes, other belongings, and crafts that the campers have completed throughout the week. Also make an announcement for next summer's program encouraging campers to return the following summer.

We have one last song to perform for you. It is the song we always use to close-out our week at camp, and it is the namesake song for our camp, Camp Granada, written and first performed by Allen Sherman in 1963.

So thank you again for coming to our closing program and we leave you with "Hello Muddah, Hello Faddah." This time (glaring at news anchors) with no interruptions.

SONG: "Hello Muddah, Hello Faddah"

Tech: *Play Hello Muddah (full accompaniment version).*

Director: *Thank parents one last time. Dismiss campers to dismissal area.*

Chapter 3

Chorale

TIMELINE AND OVERVIEW

Lesson One

Introduce "Sorida," "Sally Go Round the Sun," and verses one and two of "Hello Muddah, Hello Faddah." Also introduce campers to the concept of the script and read the script to campers from the beginning to "Aiken Drum."

Lesson Two

Teach "Funga Alafia," and continue working on "Hello Muddah, Hello Faddah," this time focusing on the chorus. Review verses one and two, and review "Sorida" and "Sally Go Round the Sun." Read the script from "Aiken Drum" to "Sally Go Round the Sun."

Lesson Three

Introduce "The Car Song" and the refrain of "Hello Muddah, Hello Faddah." Review the first sections of "Hello Muddah, Hello Faddah" and "Funga Alafia." Read the script from "Sally Go Round the Sun" to the entrance of the field reporter.

Lesson Four

Teach the final verses of "Hello Muddah, Hello Faddah." Review all songs, focusing on parts where singers need the most work.

Lesson Five

The final class is a large-group dress rehearsal including all campers, that should take place on stage or where you plan to perform your closing ceremony.

The stage should be arranged to include an area for campers to stand on risers (if available) for singing, and additional space for instruments that will be used during the performance. On the risers, campers should be arranged by team with the oldest campers in the back, and youngest campers in the front of their respective teams. This organization facilitates easier transitions between the pieces on the closing ceremony. Additional staging arrangements for the Spaced Out! theme are included in the closing ceremony script.

During the dress rehearsal, allow campers to practice all songs in the order of the closing ceremony. Also be sure to practice transitions, discuss stage etiquette, and ensure campers are ready for the closing ceremony.

TEACHING STRATEGIES

Early Elementary

Children in this age group are usually at fundamental levels of literacy. Therefore, teaching songs to young children should emphasize rote/echo techniques more than reading printed music. It is also suitable to use graphics or pictures that represent lyrics of the songs. Sometimes, simple sign language or physical gestures are also useful to help children remember lyrics.

When incorporating literacy, utilize poster-sized versions of the lyrics, or lyrics projected on a whiteboard or smartboard, with occasional references to printed music. Likewise, when references to printed music are made, it is more suitable to use a poster-sized version of the music rather than distribute sheet music to each child.

Middle Elementary

Middle elementary students encompass a wide range of literacy skills with regard to both text and music notation. Therefore, a mixed-methods teaching approach is most suitable. Utilize poster-sized versions of the sheet music (or projected on a whiteboard) in combination with printed copies of the lyrics (only) for each child. In echo activities, make frequent references to the music with regard to the pitch of a particular word, a melodic direction, rhythms of the syllables, or other concepts.

Upper Elementary

Upper elementary students are usually fully literate and should have adequate ability to read music in treble clef (given suitable elementary school music instruction). Therefore, it is suitable to distribute copies of sheet music to each child and/or project lyrics on a white board. During instruction, rely on a combination of rote and note teaching methods to include students of all music literacy levels. When referring to specific points on the music, slow the instructional pace a bit to allow all students sufficient time to find their place on the music.

The teaching strategies below are intended for larger groups with a wide array of abilities. For smaller groups or singers grouped by age/ability, teach the song in a manner more suited for their abilities.

Singing Fundamentals

Begin each singing lesson with age-appropriate fundamentals that engage students in the lesson, prepare them for the day, and warm up their voices. Incorporate breathing, posture, movement, and vocal warm-ups that include vowels, diction and articulation, and range of extensions suitable to the voice and the songs for the day.

Additional Concepts to Teach

As children learn songs for a performance, they also need to be instructed with regard to the logistics of the performance, and will need adequate time to practice these items before the performance. Some examples include how to get onto the stage and/or risers safely; how and where to stand on stage or risers; other specifics about stage behaviors.

Script Preparation

This year's closing ceremony is a parody of a 1938 radio broadcast that made listeners believe that earth was being invaded by creatures from another planet. The script for the closing ceremony, included in this packet, should be introduced to campers as they learn the songs that are part of the performance. Do not feel that you have to read the script to the campers; just introduce them to the story line and let them know when they will be singing, playing instruments, or acting.

Preview the script for lines and actions for the campers and prepare them for the basics of what to do, and how to do it. As you teach the script, do not tell campers that there will be a surprise guest at the end. Just tell them that the play ends with the Camp Granada theme song, "Hello Muddah, Hello Faddah."

"SORIDA"

Figure 3.1 Sorida. *Source*: Author

Materials Needed
None. A piano may be used to establish a sense of pitch when needed.

Performance
This song will be performed a cappella, with hand motions.

Teaching Sequence
Teach the movements of this song as you teach the melody so that the movements help campers learn the words and pitches. For *So*, have campers place their hands on their head; hands on shoulders for *ri*, and hands on hips for *da*. Soon, the campers will be able to sing this song simply by following the movements of the leader.

Begin by asking campers to do what you do (be your mirror). Sing the first syllable and place your hands on your head. Sing "ri" and move your hands to your shoulders. Sing "da" and move your hands to your hips. Improvise moving from one position to another while singing the corresponding syllable, and have the campers continue to mirror you.

Gradually begin to add rhythms by patting in the same place (head, shoulders, or hips) and singing the syllable to the rhythm of the patting. Use this technique to teach the rhythms and pitches of the last line of music. Continue until campers can sing the entire song.

Extensions
This song can be a vocal warm-up in following lessons, and to get the campers' voices and brains working. To see who is watching, hold the first fermata as long as you feel by keeping your hands on your head (students hold out "so" until you move on). You may also add fermatas to the first

"ri" and "da" before continuing with the rest of the song in tempo. You can also use this song as an improvisation activity by allowing campers, one at a time, to conduct the group using body movements in whatever order they choose.

Advanced singers can practice basic harmonies by dividing the class in half. Have one group follow your left hand, and the other group follow your right. Hold *So* with one hand as you move the other hand to get the other group to sing *ri* or *da*. Experiment with other harmony options as time allows and as your campers are able.

"SALLY GO ROUND THE SUN"

Ring Game

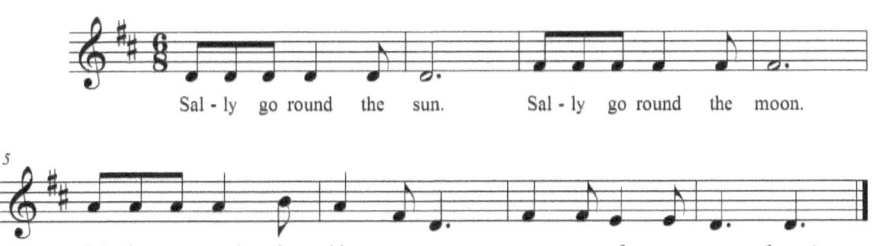

Figure 3.2 Sally Go 'Round the Sun. *Source*: Author

Materials Needed

None. A piano may be used to establish a sense of pitch when needed.

Performance

This song will be accompanied by middle elementary class using boomwhackers and other instruments. The song will be repeated four times, getting softer each time. The *boom* at the end will always be at full volume.

Teaching the Lyrics

As you teach the lyrics, have campers pat a Left Right pattern (this will reinforce what they are learning in Basics class). Teach the song using any commonly accepted rote or echo technique and continue until campers can confidently sing the entire song. Be sure the "boom" on the end is quick and somewhat loud (but not a yell).

Extensions

Movement. Have campers form a circle. You may have campers hold hands or keep hands free. Campers will walk in tempo around the circle as they sing the song. On the "boom" campers will jump up with a quick about-face and sing the song again, this time marching in the opposite direction.

For added practice, especially as campers are becoming familiar with the melody, turn this song into a freeze game. As before, have campers walk around the circle as you sing. At any random moment, stop singing and have campers freeze whenever the singing stops. The last person to freeze comes into the center of the circle and becomes the next singer. Each camper who is the last to freeze comes into the circle and sings for the next round of play. This activity will help you assess individual singers, and will provide added singing practice disguised as a game.

Dynamics. Each time the song repeats, have campers sing with a softer dynamic level. Lead campers in a brief discussion about dynamics, introducing them to *forte*, *piano*, and *diminuendo*.

For an added level of difficulty on the last repetition, have campers march in tempo around the circle while they keep the song going in their heads but do not sing with their voices. The tempo of the marching and the vocal "boom" at the end should reveal how well the tempo has stayed together. Practice the diminuendo into silence a few times to reinforce the steady beat and inner hearing.

"FUNGA ALAFIA"

Nigerian Welcome Song

Figure 3.3   Funga Alafia. *Source*: Author

Materials Needed

None. A piano may be used to establish a sense of pitch when needed.

Performance

This piece will be sung with body percussion, and accompanied by the middle elementary class on pitched percussion instruments and rhythm sticks. The campers need to be able to sing this song a cappella as there will not be a melodic accompaniment.

Teaching the Lyrics

Teach the song using any commonly accepted rote or echo technique and continue until campers can confidently sing the entire song.

Teaching the Movements

The body percussion accompaniment will include a repeated four-beat phrase shown above. Campers will need extended practice in keeping a steady beat, and with the coordination of clapping with the persons to their right and left.

Figure 3.4 **Funga Alafia Body Percussion** *Source:* **Author**

Lesson Extension

The movements of the rhythm stick pattern is identical to the body percussion movements. For beat one (floor), have campers hit the butt of the stick on the floor. For extended singing practice, allow all campers to learn and practice the rhythm stick pattern, sitting in a circle on the floor so that everyone will be able to tap with a left and right partner.

THE CAR SONG ("I'M A LITTLE PIECE OF TIN")

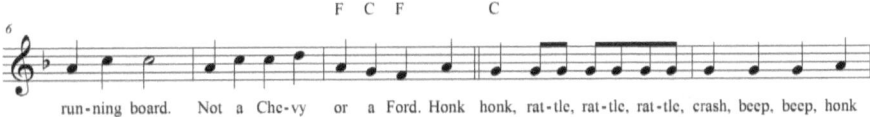

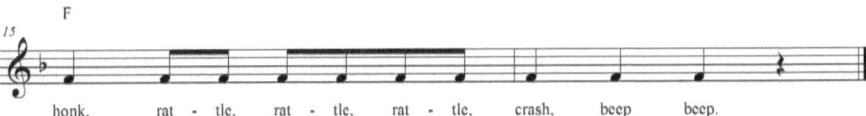

Figure 3.5 **The Car Song Melody.** *Source:* Author

78 Chapter 3

Materials Needed

None. A piano may be used to establish a sense of pitch when needed. You may also choose to have the lyrics available on a poster, white board, or projected on a screen.

Performance

This piece will be accompanied by the upper elementary class on pitched percussion and novelty instruments (trash cans, etc.) to sound like an old car. Campers should be able to sing the pitch confidently without piano accompaniment.

Teaching the Melody

Teach the song using any commonly accepted rote or echo technique and continue until campers can confidently sing the entire song. Keep the tempo slow ($\quarternote = 100$ bpm) so that the instrumentalists can perform their part in the second phrase, and the singers can clearly enunciate they lyrics.

"AIKEN DRUM"

Scottish Folk Song

[Musical notation for "Aiken Drum" with lyrics:]

There was a man lived in the moon, lived in the moon, lived in the moon. There was a man lived in the moon, and his name was Ai-ken Drum. And he played up-on a la-dle, a la-dle, a la-dle. He played up-on a la-dle and his name was Ai-ken Drum. And his _____ was made of _____ of _____. His _____ was made of _____ and his name was Ai-ken Drum. _____

Figure 2.1 Aiken Drum. *Source*: Author

NOTE—This song is used in the Starter Kit as a regularly occurring Camp Granada song, and this year it is included in the curriculum.

Performance

This song will be accompanied by the middle elementary using boomwhackers. A piano or guitar can be used for the accompaniment, but it is better if the piece is only accompanied by the boomwhackers. This is not the best key for children's voices but works best with boomwhackers and other pitched percussion.

Materials Needed

A piano may be used to establish a sense of pitch when needed, or singers may be accompanied by guitar or other harmonizing instrument. Instead of printed lyrics, draw a life-sized outline of a person (Aiken Drum) and decorate the person with the food/clothing items that the campers select. This will provide a humorous visualization to help campers remember what to sing. On the first day of camp, invite a camper to lay down on a sheet of butcher paper and outline his/her body for Aiken Drum.

Teaching the Lyrics

Teach the song using any commonly accepted rote or echo technique and continue until campers can confidently sing the entire song.

After you sing the introduction, stop and explain that Aiken Drum lives on the moon and some people like to pretend that the moon is made of cheese. In this song, people like to pretend that Aiken Drum's clothes are made of food, and the campers get to pick what food will be used to make his clothes. Beginning with the hat, encourage campers to provide types of food for each clothing item you select, and write the song based on foods provided by the campers.

Movement

Each time campers sing the chorus, have them play an air guitar.

"Hello Muddah, Hello Faddah!" (the Camp Granada Song)
Music by Lou Busch, Word by Allan Sherman © 1963 (Renewed 1991)
WB MUSIC CORP, and BURNING BUSH MUSIC

Materials Needed

Materials may vary based on the accompaniment you select for your singers. You may choose to purchase the sheet music (available from many online retailers), and have a staff member accompany singers on a keyboard instrument). There are also various audio sound tracks available for purchase online (for this you will also need a sound amplification system to accompany the singers). *Note:* For reasons of copyright law, neither the text nor the sheet music is included in this book. Both are available from online or local music retailers.

General Teaching Strategies

This song is written in such a way that it is fairly easy to teach. In the verses, the ensemble director needs to think two beats ahead of the song and whisper the words to the singers so the ensemble echos on the correct beats.

Chapter 3

A majority of the teaching time should emphasize the melody of the verses and the refrain. Again, you may use printed music or text, or poster-sized versions of the lyrics to teach this or any song.

Process

Begin by telling the children this song is a letter written to mom and dad by a boy or girl at camp. Play the Allan Sherman recording for the children and have them listen to determine:

- What has happened so far at camp?
- How much fun is the boy/girl having?
- Who has he met at camp?
- What has happened to these people?
- What does he say to try to convince mom and dad to bring him/her home?
- What happens at the end of the song?

This process will help children learn the humor of the song, and become familiar with the melody and sequence and rhyming pattern of the text.

The next step of the process can be used to teach all six verses. Speak the lyrics, in rhythm, two beats at a time, and have children echo. Continue this process for each verse.

The tricky part of this process is the last phrase of each verse. To begin, say the entire line slowly and in rhythm, and have children echo. Eventually, children will be able to complete the sentence so you will only need to provide the first words. Continue this process as needed until campers are comfortable with the lyrics of each verse.

Next, rather than speak the lyrics, sing the lyrics, two beats at a time and have children echo on pitch. Continue through each verse to teach the lyrics and melody.

Teaching the Refrain

When teaching the refrain, emphasize that notes are held out longer to sound like the boy is pleading with mom and dad to bring him home. Use any combination of rote and note techniques, similar to the way the verses were taught, to help children learn the lyrics and pitches of the refrain.

Use the refrain to teach the following concepts. In the last phrase (I've been here one whole day), the music slows down a bit. In music this is called a *ritardando*. Then, the song holds the last note out for a longer period of time (on the word "day"). In music, this is called a *fermata*. Last, there is a pause where you wait until the recording or conductor starts again. This is called a grand pause or *caesura*.

Optional Choreography

Each camper needs a 3´5 card or small sheet of paper and holds the paper down at his/her side as this song is performed. After the last phrase of the last verse, there is a short musical extension to end the song. At this point, singers pretend to write a letter on their card, crumple it up, and then toss it behind them, all tossing on the last chord (beat three) of the accompaniment.

Teaching Points

- The musical extension is 2 measures and 3 beats long.
- The first 3 beats—singers prepare by getting their papers and pretend pencils ready.
- In the first full measure, singers pretend to write their letter.
- In beats 1 and 2 of the final measure, campers crumple their letter.
- On beat 3 of the final measure (the piano's final chords), campers toss their letter.
- Tossing the letter should emphasize an upward toss, not a straight-back toss so that nobody gets hit square in the face. Singers should be allowed to practice this at least once before performing it.

SINGING GAMES

These games will provide additional singing practice for memorization, while avoiding mindless repetition of the songs. Use games with any song.

Remote Control

One child is selected to be the remote control and he or she stands in front of the group. When the child's arm is up, the group sings as normal. When the child's arm goes down, the group continues to sing the song in their heads, but no voices should be heard. When the child's arm goes back up, the group begins to sing out loud again and should all start on the same words and same pitch (the idea is, like a radio, the song continues to play when the radio is off).

Additional Options

Pick another player to stand with the remote control. This player will move his/her hands closer together or farther apart to signify how loudly or softly the group should sing. This player can move his/her hand while the group is singing, or may change the volume when the sound is off so that a new dynamic level will be performed when the song comes back on. For louder dynamics, ensure campers are singing healthily rather than screaming.

Mezzo-Screamo

This is a musical version of the well-known Hot and Cold game. One student is chosen to step outside while the group selects an object for the person to find. When the person comes back into the room, the group begins singing. As the person walks around the room, the group should sing louder or softer to show how close or far away the person is from the object. As soon as the person touches the object, the group should stop singing. Ensure children are singing, not yelling in louder dynamics.

Round Robin

Have singers stand in a large circle with one person chosen to be in the middle. This person (or the teacher) selects a song that the group will sing. The player in the middle begins by pointing to anyone on the circle who begins singing the song at the beginning. At any random time, the player in the middle points to someone else who has to keep the song going where the first person left off.

This continues until someone forgets the words or sings the wrong words. This person is now in the middle and starts over with the same song or a different song.

Teaching point: Encourage players to participate as they are comfortable, knowing that many will not want to sing alone in front of the group.

Ping Pong

(For this activity, you need a ball or beanbag.)
Have singers stand in a large circle. Toss the ball to one player who begins a song, and then tosses the ball to anyone else on the circle. This player continues the song where the first person left off and then tosses the ball to another player, and so on. This continues until the group reaches the end of the song.

Options for Play

You may choose to have each person sing only one word or an entire phrase before passing the ball. You may also choose what will happen to a player who does not know the words (be careful that what you choose does not humiliate or embarrass any player).

As a suggestion, a player who does not know the words sits down on the circle and "is out." Play continues until there is only one person left standing and this person is the winner.

Chapter 4

Basics

INTRODUCTION

In these lessons, campers will learn basic music theory as they learn to play the instrumental arrangements that accompany the songs they will learn in Chorale (singing) lessons. As such, there is time imbedded in the instrumental lessons to review singing, but this should not be the primary focus of the Basics class.

Especially in lessons one and two, campers will have had less experience with the songs and will not be as confident with regard to singing. In the first lessons of Basics class, however, it is only essential for campers to sing well enough for the purpose of the instrumental activities. Singing will improve throughout the week through additional practice in Chorale (singing class). Sheet music for the instrumental arrangements is available at the end of this section.

EARLY ELEMENTARY

Since the attention span of younger campers is considerably short, the early elementary activities are interspersed with additional teaching materials that are related to the day's theme but will not be performed on the closing ceremony.

Lesson One

In the first lesson, help children feel welcome, encourage participation, establish basic guidelines and procedures, and begin to informally assess students' prior knowledge and skills (pitch, beat, literacy).

Materials Needed

Complete set of instruments for "The Strange Visitor"

- Temple blocks and mallet
- Bass xylophone

Teaching Sequence

Icebreaker Activity (5–10 minutes)

Lead students in an introductory, icebreaker activity that will help everyone learn the names of other students in the group. For example, with campers sitting in a circle, have them begin a four-beat Pat Pat Clap [rest] pattern. Repeat this pattern as campers take turns around the circle saying their name on the clap.

"The Strange Visitor" (10–15 minutes)

"The Strange Visitor" is an English fairy tale of an old woman who meets an unexpected guest. The story is to be told using sound effects and music. The campers can either sing the reoccurring melody, or just chant the rhythm of the text. The melody is set to "Sarasponda," a Dutch spinning song. The ◀€ symbol throughout the story shows where to insert sound effects.

To begin, read the story with the campers and invite them to join you, using body percussion and voices for the sound effects. Also teach them to sing the reoccurring melody each time it appears.

Temple Block Tango (10 minutes)

Materials Needed

- Temple blocks and mallet
- Triangle (optional)

Setup. Have campers begin by sitting in a circle.

Introduction. Tell campers that they are going to march around the circle, stepping only when they hear the temple block, and freeze when the blocks stop. Begin by having campers walk with their hands (patting) to practice a bit before they try marching. Play a quarter-note walking tempo on the lowest two blocks as you say "walk" to each beat, and have the campers pat along, stopping when you stop. Play the equivalent 8th notes on the two highest blocks as you say "jogging" to the 8th notes and have campers pat along, stopping when you stop.

Play. After a few seated practice turns, have campers stand up and actually march or jog to what they hear. Allow several rounds of practice with random stops and starts, ensuring campers walk to the steady beat. You can also change the dynamics of your beat and have campers march loudly or quietly to match.

"Sally Go Round the Sun" (5–10 minutes)

Begin by teaching the campers to sing "Sally Go Round the Sun." Campers will spend more time on this in Chorale. For this activity, it is only important that they are introduced to the song. Next, add a vocal "BOOM" and one small jump after "every afternoon," and then immediately repeat the song. Have campers repeat the song four times, getting softer as they sing each time, but keeping the "boom" at full volume. As you continue, add body percussion accompaniment by inviting campers to pat the steady beat (alternating L-R) as they sing. Join them on the bass xylophone, playing the broken drone accompaniment.

Lesson Two
Materials

- Instruments for "The Strange Visitor"
- Bass xylophone
- Recording of "Head, Shoulders, Knees, and Toes" (optional)

Teaching Sequence

Introduction Activity (5 minutes)

Lead campers in "Head, Shoulders, Knees, and Toes." After the song, have campers sit down and use the song as a connection to review "The Strange Visitor." Review the story, and the body parts that came into the room.

"The Strange Visitor" (10–15 minutes)

Teach the campers about the percussion instruments that will be used in the story. Lead a brief conversation about the sounds of the instruments and which instrument is most appropriate for each sound effect in the story. Distribute instruments to campers and repeat the entire story, this time with percussion instruments, making sure every camper gets to play something. Feel free to improvise so that everyone can be involved in the performance.

Review Temple Block Tango (5–10 minutes)

Spend a few minutes reviewing the temple block tango for extra practice marching to the steady beat.

"Sally Go Round the Sun" (10–15 minutes)

Review the song and the related activities from Lesson one. Next, change the body percussion part by adding a clap after the words *sun*, *moon*, and *afternoon*. As you practice the new body percussion parts, keep the boom and jump so that, on the last beat of the song, campers clap and jump at the same time (after the word *afternoon*).

As you continue practicing with instruments, distribute hand drums and other handheld percussion instruments for campers to play instead of clap. You may also review the movement game from lesson one, and also allow some campers to try the drone part on the bass xylophone. Also continue practicing dynamics so that campers sing softer each time the song is repeated. Finally, consider allowing campers, one at a time, to try the accompaniment bass xylophone. If you do not have a suitable camper, have an intern or staff member play the drone.

Lesson Three

Materials

- Handheld percussion instruments
- Equipment for "The Strange Visitor"
- Recording of "Looby Loo" (optional)
- Open space for movement activities in lesson three.

Terms and Concepts

The movement activities in lesson three will relate to information the campers are learning in Connections class. Be sure to discuss the terms *path* and *orbit* to help campers understand the curricular connections and movement activities.

Teaching Sequence

Introductory Activity (5 minutes)

At the beginning of the session, have the line of students stop just outside the classroom door. Tell them that your drum is going to help them get in the room and they may only step when they hear the drum. (When the drum plays, they walk. When the drum stops, they stop.) Begin to play a beat with a moderate tempo as you lead the line into class, ensuring students walk (march) to the beat. At random intervals, stop the drum pattern and ensure the walking stops. Periodically change the beat (faster/slower, louder/softer, even/uneven) to teach and reinforce these aspects of the beat.

Transition Activity (5 minutes)

Lead campers in "Looby Loo." After the song, have campers sit down and use the song as a connection to review "The Strange Visitor." Review the story, the body parts that came into the room, and the sound effects or motions that accompany each body part.

"Sally Go Round the Sun" (10–20 minutes)

Arrange campers in a large circle around the largest drum and/or a bass xylophone. With larger groups, campers may be arranged in two concentric circles. Campers should not have instruments at this point.

Invite campers to march in tempo around the circle as they sing the song, accompanied by the broken drone or a steady beat on the drum. Provide ample opportunity for practice marching to the beat while singing. On the "boom" have campers jump up, turn around, and repeat the song while marching in the other direction (change directions with each repetition of the song).

After a few repetitions, discuss the vocabulary for the lesson: The word *path* means the direction you take to get from one point to another. For this song, campers should be aware of their *path* to keep the group circle from shrinking, expanding, or moving across the room. The word *orbit* means to circle around something. For this song, the *path* is an *orbit* around the drum or xylophone in the center of the circle. Invite campers to imagine they are the planets orbiting around the sun, shown by the instruments in the center of the circle.

When the campers can march to a steady tempo, in a circular path as they sing, invite them to add the clap after the words *sun*, *moon*, and *afternoon*. After a few practice tries, sing and march again with small, handheld percussion that campers can carry with them as they march. As you continue practicing, review dynamics concepts so that campers continue to sing and play their instruments more quietly each time the song is repeated.

"The Strange Visitor" (10–15 minutes)

Begin with some review questions about the story, focusing on the instruments that are used for each body part, and ensure that campers can confidently sing the melody. After review, assign parts and instruments to campers based on campers' experiences and success with instruments in lesson two. Distribute assigned instruments and run through the piece again to ensure campers know when to play and/or sing.

Lesson Four

In lesson four, you will need to finalize preparations for the closing ceremony, ensuring each camper has an assigned part to play and/or sing. It is also important to begin preparing campers for the staging and blocking transitions that take place during the script. If you can, take campers to the performance area to begin practicing where to sit, when to move, where to put instruments, and other logistics. You may need to prepare the performance area or to move instruments from the classroom space to the performance area in preparation for the day's lessons.

Materials

- Parachute (available from many music and music education supply catalogs)
- Beanbags or small balls
- Recordings of music of contrasting styles
- Recording of "Tony Chestnut" (optional)

Prepare

For the parachute and movement activities in lesson four, preselect some music of contrasting styles. You will also need a lot of open space for parachute activities. If you are unfamiliar with "Tony Chestnut," you will need to prepare yourself with the melody and the movements (audio and video recordings are available from The Learning Station).

Teaching Sequence

Introductory Activity (5 minutes)

Introduce the concept of "Tony Chestnut" by telling campers that they just have to touch a body part as it is said in the song, and that they have to listen carefully for the parts of the body *(Tony [toe–knee] Chestnut [chest–head])*. Play the song and invite campers to move along. After the song, invite campers to sit down, and use the song as a connection to review the body parts and sound effects for "The Strange Visitor."

"The Strange Visitor" (5–10 minutes)

Review "The Strange Visitor" to ensure campers know when to play and/or sing. Spend ample time practicing the transitions so that campers will know where their instruments will be, how and when in the script they are to go to their instruments, and how and when in the script they are to go back to their spots.

Parachute Activities (10–20 minutes)

These movement activities are designed to reinforce the concepts of path and orbit from lesson three, and continue preparing campers for the performance of "Sally Go Round the Sun." Specifically, these activities should ensure that the circle maintains its shape and location as campers march and sing the song.

Spread out the parachute on floor and invite campers to sit in a circle around the parachute. Once everyone has a spot, invite campers to stand up, everyone facing to the left or right, and hold the edge of the parachute with the inner hand.

Play the temple block tango activity from lesson one, this time ensuring that students march around the circle. If the parachute starts to wrinkle or lose its shape, the group is not keeping a circle. For additional help, invite campers to visualize a merry-go-round or planets orbiting the sun. Next, invite campers to march around the circle with the parachute as they sing "Sally Go Round the Sun." On each "boom," campers turn around, switch hands, and continue in the opposite direction.

Extension. Many other parachute activities are available from online teaching resources. If time permits, allow campers to participate in other parachute activities. Resource: www.playparachutes.com/pagaac.html

"Sally Go Round the Sun" (5–10 minutes)

The final concept to teach for "Sally Go Round the Sun" is the camper's ability to audiate the song while marching and playing handheld percussion instruments. With campers seated, invite them to sing as before, getting softer each time the song repeats. On the last repetition, the dynamic should be so soft that they cannot hear any voices. Instead, the campers are to internalize the song (sing it in your head) as they continue to play the drums and boom in the right place.

Once they are able to do this while sitting, invite campers to stand, form their circle around the drum or bass xylophone and practice this concept with movement. Use remaining time to practice this and any other specifics that need to be reviewed. Be sure campers know exactly how many times they will sing the song for the closing ceremony, and what they are to do with their instruments when the song is finished.

Lesson Five

On the last day, all classes will meet together for a final dress rehearsal before the closing ceremony. This will allow all students to practice on stage, and to preview the songs that other classes have prepared. Prior to the final day, you will need to move all instruments and related materials to the performance area, and arrange them on the stage.

This is an excellent opportunity to talk to students about audience etiquette, especially while they are waiting for their turn to perform. Finally, use this time to rehearse transitions from instrumental selection to singing selection and prepare students for the program.

MIDDLE ELEMENTARY

LESSON ONE

Materials

For each lesson, you will need the sheet music available at the end of this section of the book, and instruments for the accompaniment parts. For lesson one, you will also need colored dots or shapes that match the colors of the boomwhackers, arranged as shown below.

Prepare

Use an Ellison or other die-cut machine to make 3" or 4" colored dots that you will use to make a color-coded chord chart for the boomwhackers. Colors you need include red (C), orange (D), yellow (E), green (F), teal (G), purple (A), and pink (B).

Post the colored dots on a display board somewhere for the entire class to see. Be sure the dots resemble note heads, positioned vertically to resemble chords, and to represent beats in the measure (leaving an empty space for beat 2 of each measure).

NOTE: Joia tube colors do not match boomwhacker colors. If you are going to include Joia tubes, play only the roots of the chords and teach this part by note name. This will fit into step 6 of the lesson below.

Table 4.1   Boomwhacker Music

	♪ ..♪	♪ ♪	♪ ♪	♪ ♪	♪ ♪	♪ ♪	♪ ♪	♪ ♪	♪ ♪	♪ ♪	♪ ♪	♪ ♪	♪
	G	A	G	D	G	A	G	D	G
	E	F	E	B	E	F	E	B	E
	C	C	C	G	C	C	C	G	C
Joia Tube & Contra-bass Bar	C	F	C	G	C	F	C	G	C

Terms and Concepts

Use the middle elementary lessons to teach and reinforce the terms *melody* (the part of a song that you sing), *harmony* (part of a song that supports the melody), and *chords* (two or more notes played at the same time, usually to support the melody).

Teaching Sequence

In the first lesson, help children feel welcome, encourage participation, establish basic guidelines and procedures, and begin to informally assess students' prior knowledge and skills (pitch, beat, literacy).

Icebreaker Activity (5–10 minutes)

Lead students in an introductory, icebreaker activity that will help everyone learn the names of other students in the group. For example, with campers sitting in a circle, have them begin a four-beat Pat Pat Clap [rest] pattern. Repeat this pattern as campers take turns around the circle saying their name on the clap.

"Funga Alafia" (10–15 minutes)

Before you begin teaching the accompaniment, campers may need an introduction or review of the melody of "Funga Alafia." Campers will spend more time on this in Chorale, but will need basic familiarity with the melody as they learn the accompaniment. Once campers are comfortable with the melody, teach the body percussion accompaniment as *Pat Clap Clap Clap*. Practice the steady beat with campers through a variety of means, focusing on body percussion and movement.

To teach the full body percussion, invite campers to sit in a circle. Teach campers to clap their own hands on the first clap, to clap with their neighbor's hands (left and right) on the second clap, and then their own hands again for the final clap. The new pattern is *Down, In, Out, In* or *Pat, Clap, Partner* clap. Lead the song a few times for campers to practice singing while performing the clapping pattern.

"Aiken Drum" (10–15 minutes)

Before you begin teaching the accompaniment, campers may need an introduction or review of the melody of "Aiken Drum." As you teach and review the melody, use body percussion (patting) to prepare the campers for the boomwhacker parts. Invite campers to pat the rhythm of the boomwhacker part as they sing the song (pat on the first beat of each measure, and pat beats 1 and 2 of the phrase endings).

For the next step, you will need the colored dot music posted on the board or wall for campers to follow. As you are able to observe campers, try to get an idea of which campers have a stronger sense of timing. Later, these students will need to be assigned a color that repeats more frequently (any color in the one [I] chord. Point to the chords on the downbeats as campers follow the music from left to right. Assign each camper to a color and have them sing again, this time patting only when they see their color. This step may need a few repetitions for practice.

Lesson Two

Materials

- Instruments for the accompaniments
- Printed dot music for "Aiken Drum"
- Temple blocks and mallet

Teaching Sequence

Temple Block Tango (5–10 minutes)

See instructions in "Early Elementary" Basics lesson one.

"Funga Alafia" (10 minutes)

Review the song and clapping pattern from lesson one. Next, distribute rhythm sticks and teach campers the rhythm stick pattern. For beat one, have campers tap the butt of the stick on the floor; for beat two, tap sticks together; for beat three tap with your left and right neighbor (being careful not to hit fingers); and tap your own sticks together again for beat four. Allow ample time to practice this pattern, beginning slowly and gradually increasing in tempo until campers can readily perform the pattern at the tempo of "Funga Alafia."

The arrangement for "Funga Alafia" is fairly straightforward and campers may be able to perform it fairly quickly. The most difficult concepts will be the steady beat, and the coordination to perform the rhythm stick pattern. Therefore, you may need extra beat-keeping activities, and/or rhythm stick activities.

"Aiken Drum" (15–25 minutes)

Review the singing of "Aiken Drum," and the body percussion part from lesson one. Assign campers to a color to follow and have them pat only when they see their color.

Before distributing boomwhackers, it may be useful to provide a brief introduction as some may not have prior experience with the instruments. Be sure to include basic technique (where to tap the instruments) and your classroom procedures for what to tap and what not to tap. After a brief introduction, distribute boomwhackers and lead a few introductory activities to help campers learn the basic concepts of playing boomwhackers. Mainly, your activities will need to focus on the timing of getting a large group of campers all playing at the same time, and the ability of the group to keep the steady beat.

Sample Practice Activity. Divide campers into four groups, invite them to sit by groups, and distribute boomwhackers to each group. At this point, pitch does not matter. Assign one group as the starting group that will play their boomwhackers on beat one. Once this group starts, the next group will play on beat two, the next on three, and the last on four. Keep a steady beat on temple blocks, claves, or other instrument and allow time for campers to practice keeping a steady beat and playing the boomwhackers together.

Lesson Three

Materials

- Instruments for arrangements
- Dot music for "Aiken Drum"

Teaching Sequence

"Funga Alafia" (10–15 minutes)

Begin by reviewing concepts from lessons one and two of "Funga Alafia." Next, teach the bass line from the arrangement on boomwhackers, Joia tubes, or bass xylophones, and allow sufficient time for campers to practice each part. Ensure that campers continue to sing the melody as they play the accompaniment parts.

"Aiken Drum"

Theory component (10 minutes). Lead a brief discussion with campers about why certain notes are played at some times, but not at others. Use this conversation to define a *chord* as a group of two or three notes that support or accompany a melody (the part you sing). To make a chord, pick a starting or bottom note (the *root*). From there, go up the musical alphabet, picking every other letter, like counting by odd numbers (1, 3, and 5).

For group practice, write a two-octave C major scale on the board. Starting on C, invite campers to count every other letter to spell the C chord as C, E, and G. Repeat this process, starting on different notes on the scale for extended practice. Be sure you include the F and G major scales as this will be important for "Aiken Drum." For the sake of this lesson, do not differentiate between major or minor, as this is too much information for a basic lesson on chords, and is not related to "Aiken Drum."

Next, inform campers that musicians use chords to accompany or support a melody. A composer listens to the notes of the melody to select the chords that sound the best, and the most common chords are the chords that start on the first, fourth, and fifth notes of the scale, just like the chords in "Aiken Drum."

Song practice (10–15 minutes). Begin by reviewing the boomwhacker techniques and concepts from lesson two. Distribute instruments again and lead students through the song using the dot music. As a transition, sing or say the song slowly, and have campers raise their boomwhackers in the air when the song comes to their color. When campers seem confident on their parts, allow them to play the instruments as the song is performed. Repeat a few times for continued practice.

Bass line (remaining time). If you have a musically advanced group of campers, you may choose to add the bass line from the arrangement using boomwhackers or bass xylophones. In the remaining time, teach the bass part to campers and allow for a few rotations to see how well campers do with this part.

Lesson Four

In lesson four, you will need to finalize preparations for the closing ceremony, ensuring each camper has an assigned part to play and/or sing. It is also important to begin preparing campers for the staging and blocking transitions that take place during the script. If you can, take campers to the performance area to begin practicing where to sit, when to move, where to put instruments, and other logistics. You may need to prepare the performance area or to move instruments from the classroom space to the performance area in preparation for the day's lessons.

Materials

- Instruments for the arrangements
- Dot music for "Aiken Drum"

Prepare

In lesson four, begin preparing campers for the transitions that will need to happen on the closing ceremony. If you can, take campers to the performance area to begin practicing where to sit, when to move, where to put instruments, and other logistics. You may need to prepare the performance area or to move instruments from the classroom space to the performance area in preparation for the day's lesson. You will also need to begin selecting and assigning campers to perform each part in preparation for the day's lesson.

Teaching Sequence

"Funga Alafia" (15–20 minutes)

Prior to the lesson, assign campers for each part. Review the song with full accompaniment as needed, allowing ample time for campers to practice their assigned parts. If time allows, you may add non-pitched percussion to mark the endings of the phrases and select campers to play this part.

"Aiken Drum" (15–20 minutes)

Begin with a review of the prior lessons, and allow for extended practice on the bass part if you are using it. By this time in the week, the campers have selected specific items of food to use for Aiken Drum's clothes. Be sure campers are singing the correct words while performing the accompaniment.

Also, assign campers to boomwhackers and allow ample time for campers to practice playing on their assigned pitch.

Remaining Time

If time remains, review the temple block tango, parachute activities, or other games that continue reinforcing the steady beat.

Lesson Five

On the last day, all classes will meet together for a final dress rehearsal before the closing ceremony. This will allow all students to practice on stage, and to preview the songs that other classes have prepared. Prior to the final day, you will need to move all instruments and related materials to the performance area, and arrange them on the stage.

This is an excellent opportunity to talk to students about audience etiquette, especially while they are waiting for their turn to perform. Finally, use this time to rehearse transitions from instrumental selection to singing selection and prepare students for the program.

UPPER ELEMENTARY

The instrumental arrangements and related activities for the upper-elementary students are usually more complex than those for younger students. As such, it may initially appear as though there are fewer activities for older campers. However, given the complexity of the tasks, older campers will need more time to prepare their parts of the closing ceremony.

LESSON ONE

"Song for Pluto"

The "Song for Pluto" is a piece that the campers will perform throughout the week. As such, there is no sheet music for "Song for Pluto." You may choose to notate parts of the music on a whiteboard, or have campers make their own notes on scratch paper.

This piece is divided into four layers, and each layer needs a different grouping of instruments. The melody layer needs high-pitched metals, arranged for C pentatonic. Glockenspiels, resonator bell sets, and pitched desk bell sets (if available) are most suitable.

The optional harmony part needs medium-ranged metals or woods (alto metallophones and/or xylophones, also arranged for C pentatonic).

The percussion layer needs a miscellaneous array of handheld percussion instruments, and any mallets that may be needed. The bass or drone layer needs low-pitched bass or contrabass bars.

The leader (a staff member or intern) needs a whistle or other unique instrument to signal "rotate," and a gong, cymbal, or other instrument to signal "stop."

"The Car Song"

"The Car Song" can be accompanied with any array of instruments you have available. Suggestions are provided on the sheet music at the end of this section of the book, but feel free to improvise with whatever you have.

"Au Clair de la Lune"

For "Au Clair de la Lune," campers will need to see recorder melody, either copied and distributed, projected on a screen, or posted on a whiteboard. Regarding the arrangement, the toy piano part is only to provide a foundation for the arrangement, and may not be needed. It may be performed by camp staff, by a student who has prior piano experience, or may be left out.

Prepare

"Song for Pluto"

Arrange instruments on the floor in groups (melody, harmony, percussion, and bass), with enough room for a few campers to sit around each instrument cluster. Campers need to be divided into three or four groups, depending on the size of your program, and each group will sit in a circle around their assigned instruments. Each group should be small enough for campers to reach in to the center to play an instrument without moving it or picking it up. Instrument clusters should be spread out around the room with the teacher in the center.

"Au Clair de la Lune"

To prepare for "Au Clair de la Lune," ensure the recorder melody is ready to distribute to campers, or written on a whiteboard or poster, with the A and B phrases clearly labeled.

Teaching Sequence

Icebreaker Activity (5 minutes)

Lead students in an introductory, icebreaker activity that will help everyone learn the names of other students in the group. For example, with campers sitting in a circle, have them begin a four-beat Pat Pat Clap [rest] pattern. Repeat this pattern as campers take turns around the circle saying their name on the clap.

"Song for Pluto" (10 minutes)

Briefly introduce Gustav Holst's *The Planets* and the concept of this piece. Campers will receive a more thorough introduction to this piece in Connections class. For the purposes of this lesson, campers need to know that when Holst wrote *The Planets*, Pluto had not yet been discovered so there is no piece for Pluto; and that their task for the week is to compose a "Song for Pluto."

Invite campers to sit in one large circle with the teacher in the center. Designate one camper as the starting point (this can change as needed). Tell campers that you are going to play a slow, steady beat on the drum. The starting camper will clap on a beat. The next camper will clap on the next beat, and this will continue as the beat moves around the circle, one camper at a time.

Help campers understand this is not a race, or a game of hot potato. Each person must clap on the next beat as it goes around the circle. It may help to have campers count a steady beat like they are numbering off for a team game (1, 2, 3, 4).

As the group gains confidence in this skill, invite campers to experiment with other things to do on their turn. Some may choose to pat their heads, snap, or perform some other (appropriate) body percussion. Some may also choose to perform a pair of 8th notes on their beat. Later, add the option of a quarter rest. For this addition, campers must do something to physically show a silent beat on their turn. As an optional rule, tell campers that they may not choose the same thing as the person before them. Continue for a few practice rounds to help campers gain confidence in this skill.

"The Car Song" (10–15 minutes)

Before you begin teaching the instrumental accompaniment, campers may need an introduction or review of the melody of "The Car Song." Campers will spend more time on this in Chorale, but will need basic familiarity with the melody as they learn the instrumental parts.

Teach/review the melody so that campers are confident singing the song as they play percussion or perform body percussion. As you practice the singing, add the body percussion ostinato from the arrangement, and allow ample practice time.

"Au Clair de la Lune" (10–20 minutes)

Provide a brief introduction to this piece as a French folk song about moonlight. Demonstrate the melody on recorder (A phrase) and glockenspiel (B phrase), and invite campers to describe the melody and its mood.

Next, demonstrate the drone (bass metallophone part) and invite campers to use body percussion to mirror your movements. The body percussion movement should introduce the cross-*over left-right-left* movement needed to perform the part, and should prepare campers to play the part on instruments.

Before transitioning to the instruments, it may be useful to introduce campers to the procedures and basic techniques of playing barred instruments, depending on their prior experiences. After an introduction, transition the body percussion movements to the drone part and allow time for campers to practice the drone in tempo. Finally, allow campers to play the drone as you (or an assistant) demonstrate the melody on recorder, glockenspiel, or other instrument.

Lesson Two

Materials Needed

- Instruments for arrangements
- Music for "Au Clair de la Lune" (optional)
- Music for "Song for Pluto" (optional)

Prepare

If you are using the same recorders each day, be sure they are cleaned, or labeled so that each camper uses the same recorder throughout the week. You may also encourage campers to bring their own recorders from home.

Teaching Sequence

"Song for Pluto" (10 minutes)

Begin with a review of the beat-keeping activity from lesson one. Next, divide the class into smaller groups and have each group form a circle. Designate one camper per group as the starting point in each circle (this can change as needed). Repeat the activity as before, but with multiple circles performing at the same time. The trick now is that campers will hear the beats and rhythms being created by other circles, while still trying to focus on their own group.

Next, distribute non-pitched percussion instruments to each group and repeat the activity, this time using instruments instead of body percussion. Continue to enforce the concept that campers may not choose the same instrument or rhythm as the person before them. The leader may need to keep a steady tempo on claves, a cow bell, or other obvious instrument to keep groups together and reinforce the steady beat.

"The Car Song" (10 minutes)

Begin with a review of the melody and body-percussion ostinato from lesson one. Replace the body-percussion pattern with the instruments you selected for the engine sound effects in phrase A. Repeat phrase A to allow campers to practice performing the instrument accompaniment while singing.

"Au Clair de la Lune" (20–25 minutes)

Teach campers to play phrase A on the recorder. The pace for this part of the lesson will differ based on the prior experiences of your campers. While some students may have experience with recorder, there may be others who have not yet played the instrument and will need a brief introduction. Some general guidelines include:

- Make sure all students know how to hold the instrument correctly (left hand on the top holes).
- Make sure all students know how to blow into the instrument correctly to get a characteristic sound.
- Make sure all students know the procedures for when it is time to play and when it is time to stop.

You may also need to take some time to teach the fingerings for the notes G, A, and B. Some general guidelines include:

- Teach one fingering (one note) at a time and allow plenty of time for practice.
- As new notes and fingerings are introduced, allow plenty of time for students to practice the transitions from one note to another.

As students are ready, begin reading through and practicing phrase A of "Au Claire," assisting as needed. Once students are able to play through the entire A phrase, allow campers to rotate from the drone on barred instrument to the melody on recorder so that they can practice both. You may also choose to allow campers to perform the melody on a barred instrument. Rotate campers and repeat as needed to provide additional ensemble practice, and reinforce the steady beat.

Lesson Three

Materials Needed

- Instruments for arrangements
- Music for "Au Clair de la Lune" (optional)
- Music for "Song for Pluto" (optional)

Prepare

Ensure barred instruments for are set for C pentatonic for "Song for Pluto," and have the F# bars ready for "Au Clair de la Lune."

Teaching Sequence

"Song for Pluto" (10–15 minutes)

Begin with a review of the concepts from lessons one and two. Next select one of the smaller groups of campers to demonstrate the melody layer of this piece. This group of campers should sit in a circle centered around a glockenspiel, resonator bell set, or desk bells arranged for C pentatonic. The leader/teacher will keep a steady beat on a drum as before, but this time, campers are to play a pitch on the instrument as the beat goes around the circle. Tell campers that they may not play the same pitch as the camper before them. Also, campers may also choose to rest or play 8th notes, but each beat must be rhythmically different than the one before it.

Next, divide campers into small groups, each with their own set of resonator bars and allow time for practice. If enough instruments or mallets are not available for the entire group, campers can practice using paper xylophone templates (available online, or in the last page of this section of the book). Allow sufficient time for campers to practice the skill of recognizing the pitch and rhythm performed by the camper before them, and instantly choosing to play something different.

Distribute pitched instruments to some groups and non-pitched percussion to others and allow time for a few rotations so campers get to practice both parts. This step should begin to sound like an ensemble performance.

"The Car Song" (5–10 minutes)

Begin with a review of the concepts from lessons one and two. Next, teach the body percussion part for phrase B. This may require a lot of practice so start with a slow tempo and gradually work your way to performance tempo.

The instrument part for phrase B mirrors the body percussion part. Distribute instruments to campers and have them sit in the order shown on the music. Starting with a very slow tempo, teach campers to play the correct instrument at the appropriate time. Allow time for several rotations so that each camper has an opportunity to try a few instruments while others continue practicing the body percussion. While you are rotating campers through parts, try to get a sense of which campers are stronger on the body percussion, on instruments, or on one of the parts in phrase A.

"Au Clair de la Lune" (10–15 minutes)

Begin by reviewing the recorder melody (phrase A) of "Au Clair de la Lune." As you prepare to teach the B phrase, students will need a quick overview of the terms *key signature* and *sharp*. Teach a *sharp* as a music symbol (#) that makes a note sound a little higher (the black keys on a piano). Teach a *key signature* as a marking on the music that tells the musician what sharps to play (if any).

A piano keyboard has all of the notes, but the barred instruments only have the regular (or *natural*) notes. To play music that has sharps, we have to take off the natural note (bar) and put the correct sharp. *Au Clair* uses F# instead of regular F so we have to put the F# bar on the glockenspiel to play this phrase.

Once the instruments are ready, teach campers to play the B phrase on glockenspiels (measures eight through eleven), and allow ample time for practice. If time permits, begin practicing the transition from phrase A (on recorder) to B (glockenspiel).

Lesson Four

In lesson four, you will need to finalize preparations for the closing ceremony, ensuring each camper has an assigned part to play and/or sing. It is also important to begin preparing campers for the staging and blocking transitions that take place during the script. If you can, take campers to the performance area to begin practicing where to sit, when to move, where to put instruments, and other logistics. You may need to prepare the performance area or to move instruments from the classroom space to the performance area in preparation for the day's lessons.

Materials Needed

- Instruments for arrangements
- Music for "Au Clair de la Lune" (optional)
- Music for "Song for Pluto" (optional)

Teaching Sequence

"Song for Pluto" (10–15 minutes)

In lesson three, campers should have been introduced to the melody and percussion layers of "Song for Pluto." Begin by dividing campers into their Pluto groups, and reviewing the concepts from lesson three.

Next, distribute the bass instruments to one of the groups (contrabass bar [C], bass xylophone, or bass drum). Teach this group that they will not play on every beat of the measure; but instead, all members of this group will play together on the first beat of each measure. For this part, remind campers of the beat-keeping activity from lesson one (counting 1, 2, 3, 4) and encourage them to count silently together as a group to help each other play only on beat one.

Put all parts together and allow campers time to practice playing in the full ensemble. With a larger class, add a harmony cluster that uses alto instruments or boomwhackers instead of soprano instruments. Given the quick nature of this piece, have campers strike boomwhackers with a yarn mallet rather than try the traditional technique.

The last step in "Song for Pluto" is to add a rotation so that everyone gets a chance to play every part. For this step, the teacher will need to perform a one-measure rhythm pattern on a unique instrument that is easy to hear (a whistle or cowbell, for instance). This measure will signal to the campers that it is time to rotate.

To begin, assign campers to a starting group, and assign a camper in each group who will play first. At the starting signal (performed by the teacher), the first camper in each group will initiate the beat that continues around the circle. After a suitable amount of time (4 to 8 measures), the teacher will play the *rotate* pattern on the chosen instrument, followed by a four-measure improvisation pattern on a drum. Campers use this four measures to rotate groups (one group to the right) and get set for the next round of play. Rotations continue until all campers have been in all groups. The piece ends by the teacher play the gong or cymbal crash to signal the end.

"The Car Song" (5–10 minutes)

Assign campers to parts and begin to practice the full ensemble. Repeat as needed.

"Au Clair de la Lune" (10–20 minutes)

Begin by reviewing "Au Clair de la Lune" from the first few lessons. As you begin to see campers' strengths, assign them to a part in which they will be most successful. Slowly begin to piece the song together by playing phrase A, and then phrase B.

Use basic music theory terminology to make final preparations for this piece. Teach the definition of a *phrase* as a part of a song, like sentences in a paragraph. Next, teach the definition of *form* as the patterns of the *phrases* in a song.

The form of "Au Clair de la Lune" is AABA where the recorder part is phrase A, and the glockenspiel part is phrase B. This tells the performer to play the recorder part two times, the glockenspiel part one time, and then to finish with one more repetition of the recorder part.

Finally, assign campers to parts and allow for extended practice, solving problems as needed. As a decorative layer to the texture, add the finger cymbal part (can also be played on a triangle).

Lesson Five

On the last day, all classes will meet for a final dress rehearsal before the closing ceremony. This will allow all students to practice on stage, and to preview

Basics

the songs that other classes have prepared. Prior to the final day, you will need to move all instruments and related materials to the performance area, and arrange them on the stage.

This is an excellent opportunity to talk to students about audience etiquette, especially while they are waiting for their turn to perform. Finally, use this time to rehearse transitions from instrumental selection to singing selection and prepare students for the program.

SHEET MUSIC FOR BASICS LESSONS

"The Strange Visitor"
Materials Needed

Table 4.2 "The Strange Visitor" Instrument Table

Word Cue	Instrument Suggestion	Voices and Body Percussion
The wind blew	Whirly tube(s)	Voices: "whoooo"
The lightning flashed	Cymbals	Voices: tshhh—tshhh
The thunder boomed	Thunder tube or bass drum roll	Feet quickly stomping on floor
And the rain poured	Rain stick	Hands quickly patting on legs
And the door opened	Voices: "Reeeeeeee" Arm: opening door motion	Voices: "Reeeeeeee" Arm: opening door motion
And the door shut	Slap stick	One loud clap
Feet	Big drum (marching sound)	Feet: Stomp! Stomp!
Legs	Springy door stop	Hands: Pat! Pat!
Body	Ratchet or cabasa	Maracas or shakers
Head	Voices: a short scream	Voices: a short scream
Monster/Alien sound	Children's voices imitating an alien or monster	

The Melody

Campers are to sing this melody each time indicated in the script.

[Adaptation of Sarasponda]

Figure 4.1 The Strange Visitor Melody. *Source*: Author

Narrator: A woman was sitting at her wheel one night, waiting for a friend to come.

Campers: *Sing melody*

Narrator: And the wind blew, 🔉 and the door opened. 🔉 In came a pair of really big feet, and plopped down on the floor. 🔉 "How strange!" said the old woman, and she shut the door. 🔉

Campers: *Sing melody*

Narrator: And the wind blew, 🔉 and the lightning flashed, 🔉 and the door opened. 🔉 In came a pair of small (furry) legs, 🔉 and sat down on the really big feet 🔉 that had plopped down on the floor. "How strange!" said the old woman, and she shut the door 🔉

Campers: *Sing melody*

Narrator: And the wind blew, 🔉 and the lightning flashed, 🔉 and the thunder boomed, 🔉 and the door opened. 🔉 In came a big, fat, jiggly body 🔉 that plopped itself on the furry legs 🔉 that had plopped themselves on the big, fat feet 🔉 that had plopped down on the floor. "How strange!" said the old woman, and she shut the door 🔉

Campers: *Sing melody*

Narrator: And the wind blew, 🔉 and the lightning flashed, 🔉 and the thunder boomed, 🔉 and the rain poured, 🔉 and the door opened. 🔉 In came a big, ugly head 🔉 that sat down on the big, fat, jiggly body 🔉 that plopped itself on the furry legs 🔉 that had plopped themselves on the big, fat feet 🔉 that had plopped down on the floor. "How strange!" said the old woman, and she shut the door 🔉

Narrator: The old woman turned to the strange visitor and asked: How did you get such big feet?

Campers: *Make nonsense sounds and grunts like an alien or monster trying to communicate.*

Narrator: How did you get such small, furry legs?

Campers: *Nonsense sounds*

Narrator: How did you get such a big body?

Campers: *Nonsense sounds*

Narrator: How did you get such a huge head?

Campers: *Nonsense sounds*

Narrator: *Nonsense sounds*

Campers: (*loudly*) **For you!**

The Strange Visitor. *Source*: Author

"SALLY GO ROUND THE SUN"

arr. Eric Branscome

Figure 4.2 Sally Go Round the Sun. *Source*: Author

"FUNGA ALAFIA"

arr. Eric Branscome

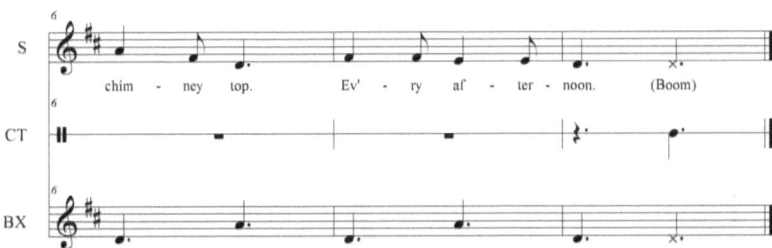

Figure 4.3 Funga Alafia. *Source*: Author

Figure 4.4 **Aiken Drum.** *Source*: Author

"AU CLAIR DE LA LUNE"

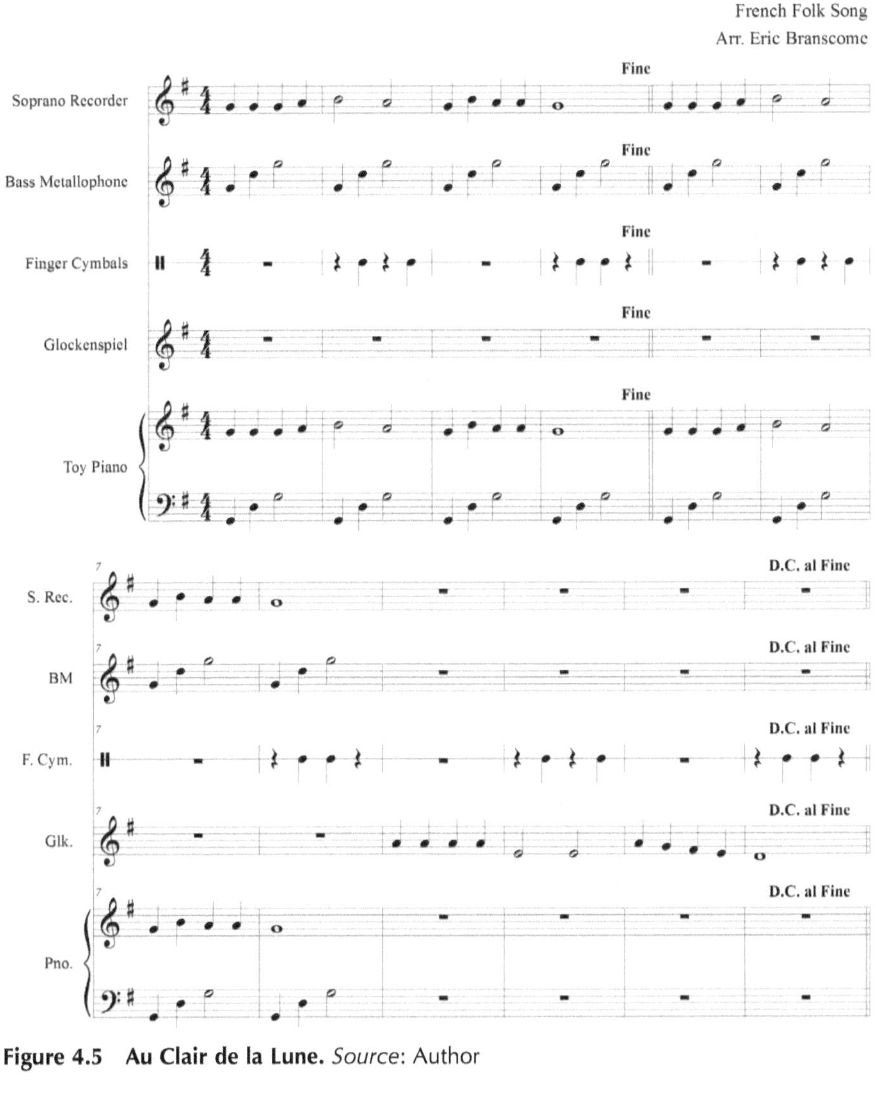

Figure 4.5 Au Clair de la Lune. *Source*: Author

110 *Chapter 4*

"THE CAR SONG

Traditional Song
Arr. Eric Branscome

Figure 4.6a **The Car Song.** *Source*: Author

Basics

Figure 4.6b The Car Song. *Source*: Author

PAPER XYLOPHONE TEMPLATE

Copy and distribute as needed for silent practice when there are not enough xylophones.

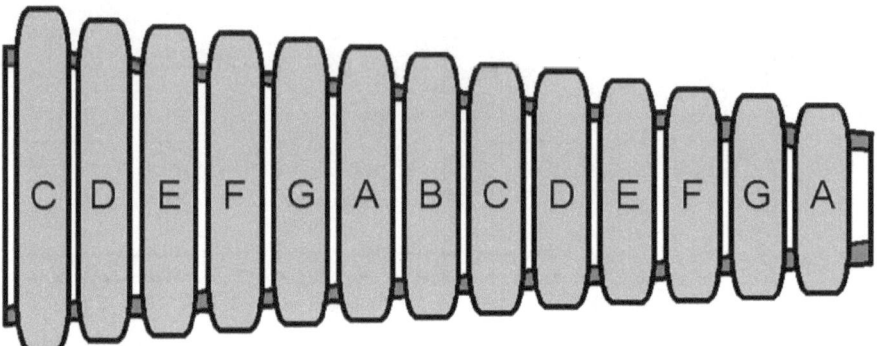

Figure 4.7 **Xylophone template.** *Source*: Author

Chapter 5

Connections

Connections lessons build upon skills and concepts that have been introduced in Chorale and Basics lessons through listening, movement, and art activities. For the closing ceremony, you may wish to decorate the stage with students' art projects, or display projects on tables in a lobby or other public place. The extension activity will serve as the backdrop on stage for the closing ceremony. At the end of the closing ceremony, all students should be allowed to retrieve their projects to take them home.

Templates for each activity are provided in the instructions. Some templates may need to be enlarged to match the dimensions described in the instructions. Prior to the start of camp, print and copy templates as needed, and make a sample of each activity to display in the Connections room.

Some projects may be completed in one day while others will take two or days to complete. Follow the suggested daily schedule to keep campers on target. An extension activity has also been included as a project for campers to complete whenever they finish their project earlier than other campers.

DAILY SCHEDULE

Day One
Early and Middle Elementary: Make the satellite kazoo
Upper Elementary: Introduction to Gustav Holst's *The Planets*, listen to *Mercury*, and begin Mission Control (coloring only).

Day Two
Early and Middle Elementary: Make the UFO Shaker, and begin Alien Mask (introduction, design, and sketching only).

114   *Chapter 5*

Upper Elementary: Listen to *Venus* and *Mars* from *The Planets*. Alien Mask (introduction, design, and sketching only). Use remaining time to continue coloring Mission Control.

Day Three
Early and Middle Elementary: Begin with day one of the Eric Carle Solar System. Spend remaining time on the Face Explorer.

Upper Elementary: Begin with the first steps of the Eric Carle Solar System. Listen to *Jupiter* and *Saturn* from *The Planets*. Spend remaining time cutting and assembling the Mission Control project.

Day Four
Early and Middle Elementary: Begin with day two of the Eric Carle Solar System, and then use remaining time to complete the Face Explorer, and Alien Masks.

Upper Elementary: Color and assemble Floating in Space. Finish the Eric Carle Solar System. Use remaining time to listen to *Neptune* and *Uranus*, review *The Planets*.

SATELLITE KAZOO

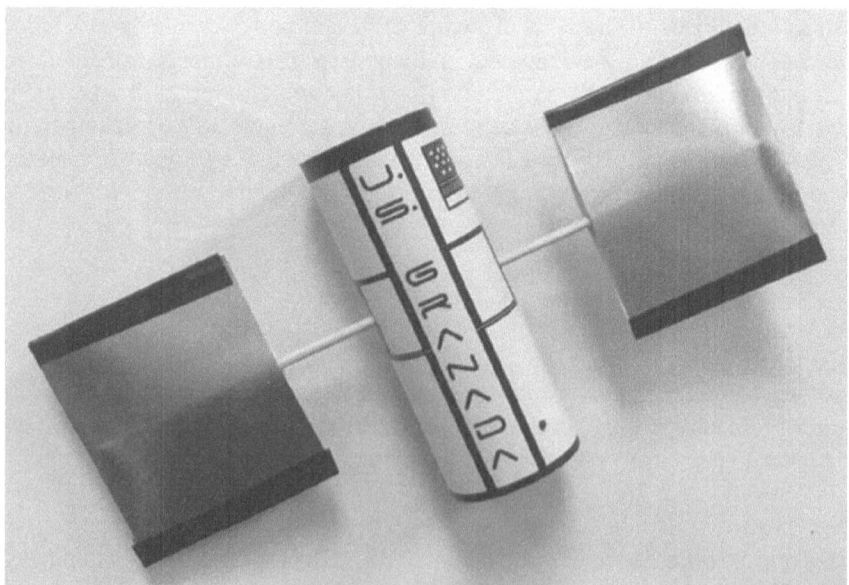

Figure 5.1 Satellite Complete. *Source*: Author

Materials Needed

- Cardboard roll for each camper (the size of a recycled toilet paper roll—one per camper)
- Satellite template (one per camper)
- Wooden cooking skewer (one per camper)
- Heavy-duty cutters (to cut the skewers)
- 4" × 4" piece of wax paper (one per camper)
- Rubber bands (one per camper)
- Single-hole punch
- Scotch tape
- Silver poster board (enough for each camper to have two pieces, each measuring 3" × 5")
- Crayons or makers
- Scissors
- Optional: decorative tape (washi tape, colored gaffers tape, or small, colored masking tape). This tape should be no wider than 1/2" across.

Prepare

Copy the satellite templates.
Cut wax paper and poster board into the required sizes.

Introduction

Although the kazoo is a simple instrument, some campers may need a brief introduction that they are to sing through, not blow into, a kazoo.

Teaching Sequence

To make the satellite body, distribute a satellite template to each camper. Make crayons or markers available and allow enough time for campers to design and color their satellites. As campers are coloring, distribute toilet-paper tubes, wax paper, and rubber bands.

When campers are finished coloring, have them set the colored templates aside. Next, have campers cover one end of the toilet-paper tube with the wax paper and use the rubber band to hold the paper in place.

Next, either tape or glue the satellite template around the toilet-paper tube.

Use a single-hole punch to make a hole in one end of the tube to allow air to escape when the kazoo is played.

To make the solar panels, use a pin or small nail to poke a hole about halfway down the tube and make sure the hole goes through both sides. Push the wood skewer through the tube so it sticks out on both the sides. Cut off the excess so there are about 4" on both the sides of the tube.

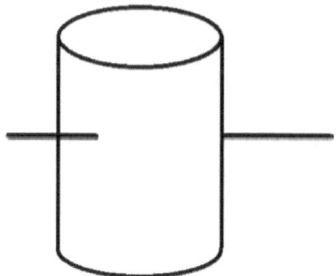

Figure 5.2 Satellite Step 1. *Source*: Author

Fold the two 3" × 5" sections of silver poster board in half, width-wise with the silver side out, and tape the inside of the poster board to the skewer. Fold the sections the rest of the way down and staple or tape into place. For decorative effect, line the side of each solar panel with decorative tape.

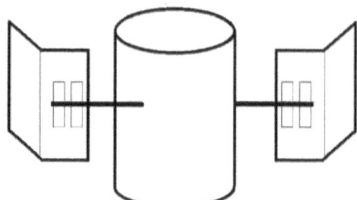

Figure 5.3 Satellite Step 2. *Source*: Author

Satellite Kazoo Template

- Copy one template for each camper, and enlarge to ensure that the printed dimensions are 4.5" high by 5.5" long.

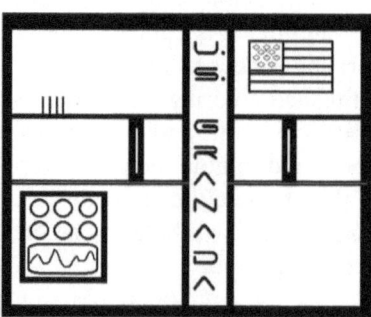

Figure 5.4 Satellite Template. *Source*: Author

UFO SHAKER/OCEAN DRUM

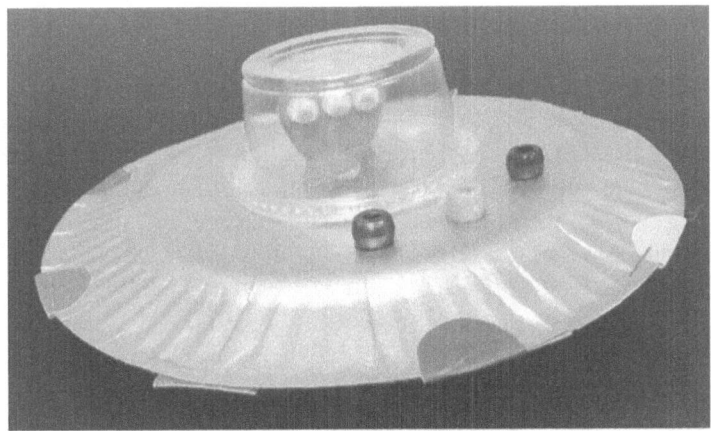

Figure 5.5 UFO Shaker Complete. *Source*: Author

Materials Needed

- 6" paper (not styrofoam) plates (enough for each camper to have two)
- Condiment cup (small, clear plastic cup with lid, usually in the condiment aisle of a local grocery store)
- Markers, crayons, and/or silver spray paint
- Craft beads
- Tape, glue, stapler, and/or garage sale sticker dots
- Plastic craft beads, or dried beans
- Small google eyes
- Small (1") pom-poms
- Hot glue gun/glue (optional but recommended)

Prepare

For an authentic looking UFO, spray paint the paper plates silver with enough time for the paint smell to dissipate before you give plates to the campers. Since spray paint can melt styrofoam, it is important to use paper plates.

Introduction

Campers are usually familiar with shakers but may not know about an ocean drum. Demonstrate the concept of an ocean drum by dropping a small handful of beads into a frame drum or hand drum and rolling it around so campers can hear/see the effect of slowly swirling around the beads.

Teaching Sequence

Distribute two paper plates to each camper and allow them time to color their plates to look like a UFO. While campers are coloring their plates, give each camper a small handful of beads. When campers are done coloring, they will place the beads in one plate, and then set the other plate on top to make the body of the UFO. Glue, tape, or staple around the edges. Colored garage sale sticker dots make a colorful addition to this project, resembling flashing lights.

To make the top, glue the condiment cup lid face up in the center of the top plate (this works best with hot glue, which will require adult assistance). When you are ready, the condiment cup will snap into the lid to make the top of the UFO. Before you complete the UFO, glue google eyes onto a small pom-pom and glue it into the top to look like an alien inside the UFO.

FLOATING IN SPACE

Figure 5.6 Floating in Space Complete. *Source*: Author

Introduction

This project is intended to look like the campers are floating away through space, and it teaches depth perception and three-dimensional drawing.

Materials Needed

- Black butcher paper (large enough to display each camper's painting)
- 24" × 18" white paper (one sheet per camper)

- Pencils
- Black markers
- Colored markers, crayons, or tempura paint/brushes
- Scissors
- Glue

Teaching Sequence

Distribute a black marker and sheet of white paper to each camper. Have campers stand on the paper with their shoes very near the bottom of the paper. Campers will also place their hands down on the paper, near the outside edges of the paper. Have campers trace the outlines of their hands and feet on the paper (some may need help to trace their dominant hand).

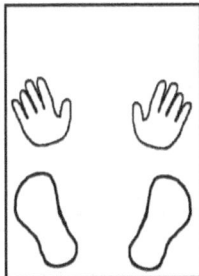

Figure 5.7 Floating in Space Step 1. *Source*: Author

Next, have campers draw their head in the top, center of the paper, and then draw in the rest of the body. For this step, you will need to demonstrate the concept of drawing arms and legs to look as though they are getting closer to the viewer toward the hands and feet. This is accomplished by starting bigger (near the hands and feet), and getting smaller toward the body. The body will be drawn smaller than usual to give the appearance of being farther away.

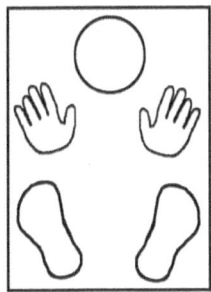

Figure 5.8 Floating in Space Step 2. *Source*: Author

Next, draw in the face and hair. Encourage campers to think about what their hair would look like in space (similar to the way their hair looks under water). Also encourage campers to think about their facial expression if they were truly floating away, and draw an appropriate face. Encourage campers to add designs, specifically to include the designs of the bottom of their shoes, patterns on their clothes, and other details on their project, and allow campers to fill in the details.

Figure 5.9 Floating in Space Step 3. *Source*: Author

FACE EXPLORER

Figure 5.10 Face Explorer Complete. *Source*: Author

Introduction

This project teaches campers to listen for and recognize mood in music. Although the concept can be used with any type of music, this project will specifically introduce younger campers to the sections of Gustav Holst's *The Planets*.

Materials Needed

- Recording of Gustav Holst's *The Planets* or alternate listening excerpts and speaker doc
- One sheet of black 9□ × 12□ construction paper per camper
- One spinner template per camper (see page 124)
- Crayons
- Metal brads (one per camper)
- Extra construction paper colors (can be small scraps)
- Star stickers (optional)
- Hole punch (or something to poke a hole in the paper)
- Pencils
- Mirrors (optional)

Prepare

For younger campers, it is helpful to precut the center circle from the face mask of the astronaut suit templates so the faces on the spinner will show through.

Teaching Sequence

This project begins with a brief introduction to the concept that music can sound happy, sad, angry, or can portray many other emotions. Play a few excerpts of contrasting music to help campers understand and get experience with this concept. Some suggestions include Bach's *Toccata in D Minor* (angry or scary), the *Funeral March*, or the second movement of Beethoven's *Seventh Symphony* (sad), or the *Can Can* melody from Offenbach's *Orpheus in the Underworld* (happy or excited).

Next, give campers some scrap paper and a pencil, and allow them time to practice drawing faces that represent a range of emotions. It may be useful to let them view some common emoticons and/or let them view their faces in a mirror to see what their eyes, eyebrows, mouths, and other parts of their faces do as they act happy, scared, sad, or other emotions.

Distribute a spinner template and a pencil to each camper. Tell campers that they will hear six examples of music that may sound happy, sad, or some other emotion and they are to draw a face to match what they hear in each circle on the spinner. Be sure campers rotate their spinner each time so that they are drawing in the top circle of the spinner and that the face is in line with the diameter of the circle.

Play six different styles of music for campers to listen and draw a face that matches in the six different faces on the spinner. Ideally, this should involve Holst's *The Planets*, using the excerpts listed below; however, these excerpts may be too musically complex for young listeners. For younger campers, consider using the alternate list of excerpts:

Table 5.1 Gustav Holst's *The Planets* Excerpts

Movement	Emotion/face	Excerpt
Mars (war)	Anger	Play first, loud phrase after the introduction, or the ending brass chords
Venus (peace)	Calm, relaxed	Opening measures
Mercury (winged messenger)	Hurried, frantic	Opening measures
Jupiter (Jollity)	Happy	Main theme (approximately one minute into the movement)
Saturn (old age)	Sleepy	Opening measures
Uranus (magician)	Scared/sneaky/worried	Opening measures

Alternate Excerpts

Table 5.2 Face Explorer Alternate Excerpts

Emotion	Excerpt
Happy	*Jump in the Line* by Harry Belafonte
Sad	Beethoven *Symphony 7, Movement 2* (opening)
Angry	Mussorgsky's *Night on Bald Mountain* (opening)
Scared	*Finlandia* (opening) by Greig
Surprised	Second movement of Symphony No. 94 (Surprise) by Haydn (opening)
Sleepy/content	*Morning from Peer Gynt* by Grieg

Once campers have drawn in their faces, allow time for campers to color the faces. While campers are coloring, distribute the astronaut suit template and allow campers to color the astronaut suits.

When everything is colored, campers will cut out the large-face template (not the individual faces), and will also cut out the astronaut suit template. Younger campers may need help with detailed cuts. Set these aside.

Give each camper a sheet of 9" × 12" black construction paper. Fold the paper in ½ (width-wise—like making a greeting card). Allow campers to pick another color of construction paper to cut out the ½ circle template. This will be glued to the bottom of the front side of the black paper to look like the astronaut is standing on a planet.

Glue the astronaut suit to the front of the paper. Be sure the astronaut is centered in the sheet of paper. Campers may need some help cutting a hole in the black paper that matches the hole in the astronaut's face shield on the helmet.

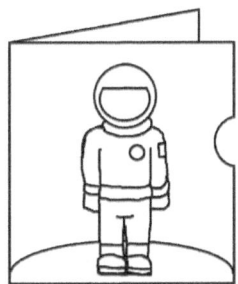

Figure 5.11 **Face Explorer Step 1.** *Source*: Author

Next cut a small half circle in the top and bottom sheets of black paper. This will allow campers to reach the spinner once it is assembled. This half circle should line up approximately with the patch on the astronaut suit's left arm.

Punch a hole in the + on the astronaut suit, making sure the hole pierces all the way through the suit and both layers of construction paper. Also poke a hole through the center of the spinner template.

Place the spinner between the two layers of black paper and insert the metal brad to hold it in place. If done correctly, this should allow the faces to appear in the face shield when the spinner is rotated.

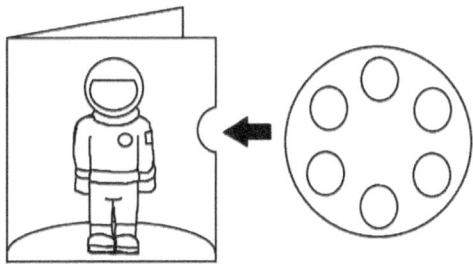

Figure 5.12 **Face Explorer Step 2.** *Source*: Author

Lesson Extension

Once the projects are assembled and completed, play the music excerpts again and invite campers to use their completed projects to show the mood they hear in the music. You may also use new excerpts to allow campers to apply the concept to new music.

Astronaut Suit Template

- Copy and enlarge to ensure printed dimensions are approximately 7.5" in length.

Figure 5.13 Face Explorer Suit Template. *Source*: Author

Astronaut Face Spinner Template

- Copy and enlarge to ensure printed dimensions are approximately 5.5" in diameter.

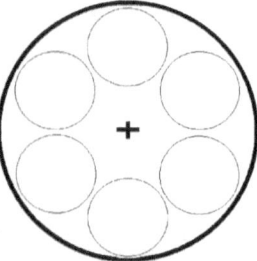

Figure 5.14 Face Explorer Spinner Template. *Source*: Author

Planet Template

- Copy and enlarge to ensure printed dimensions are approximately 6" in width by 2" in height.

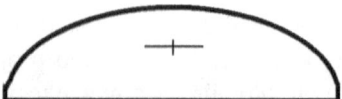

Figure 5.15 Face Explorer Planet Template. *Source*: Author

MISSION CONTROL

Overview

This project teaches campers about Holst's *The Planets*, and can be used to teach, review, and assess their knowledge of the music throughout the week. This can also be used to teach campers the basics of each planet in the solar system.

Materials

- Mission control templates (one per camper)
- Planets circle templates (one per camper)
- Card-stock paper
- Metal brads (four per camper)
- Crayons, markers, or color pencils
- Photographs or pictures of each planet (can be from any suitable children's book on astronomy or the solar system)
- Recording of Gustav Holst's *The Planets* and speaker system
- Scissors
- Hole punch

Prepare

Copy the templates onto card-stock paper. If card-stock paper, the templates can be glued onto file folders or sheets of poster board that have been cut to size. You may want to obtain a children's book on the solar system or conduct your own research on the planets. You may also want to make a word wall or other classroom display for use throughout the week of the terminology associated with this music.

Teaching Sequence

Provide a brief introduction to Holst's *The Planets*. The piece is written in seven sections and each section is supposed to sound like one of the planets (Pluto was not discovered when this piece was written, and Holst decided not to write a piece for Earth). Invite campers to consider how Holst may have decided to make each movement sound by asking "If you were going to write a piece of music for a planet, what would you want to know about the planet to help you write the song?"

After a few minutes of discussion, introduce campers to some basic information about the planet Mercury. It is the closest planet to the sun so it has the fastest orbit. It was named after an ancient Greek character who had wings on his ankles. Mercury was a messenger, and flew very fast to deliver messages.

Play the opening phrases of Holst's *Mercury* movement and lead a discussion on the sound of the piece (hurried, fast, frantic). Teach the musical term for this tempo marking, *vivace*, meaning very fast.

Distribute the circle and mission-control templates on the following pages, and allow campers to color the mission-control visual, and the planets on the first circle. Campers will need some sort of visual to know how to color each planet.

When campers are finished coloring, cut out the four triangle-shaped wedges on the mission-control template. Punch holes on the four X marks on the template, and in the center of each circle. Use the brads to connect the circles to the back of the paper. This should allow the words or pictures to show through the wedges. Be sure that campers put the circles on the correct side so that words are right-side-up in the windows. Be sure campers write their names on the back of their projects.

Lesson Extension

Throughout the week, provide brief introductions to the other sections of the music and play excerpts of each movement for the campers, relating each movement's sound to the characteristics of the planets and the Greek or Roman character after whom it was named. Be sure to teach the dynamics, tempo, or stylistic terminology associated with each movement, and encourage campers to use their projects as teaching aides as you introduce each planet. On the last day of Connections, use the completed projects as an assessment tool (game) to see how well campers remember each movement and the musical terms to describe the music.

Play excerpts that you have used throughout the week as campers listen, and use their projects to identify the elements of music. Invite campers to turn the spinners so that the correct words appear in the windows, and use the elements to identify the movements as they are played.

Mission-Control Template

- Copy and enlarge to ensure printed dimensions are 8.5" x 11".

Mission-Control Spinner Templates

Printed dimensions of each circle should be approximately four inches in diameter.

The planets on the spinner are (1) Mercury, (2) Venus, (3) Mars, (4) Jupiter, (5) Saturn, (6) Uranus, and (7) Neptune.

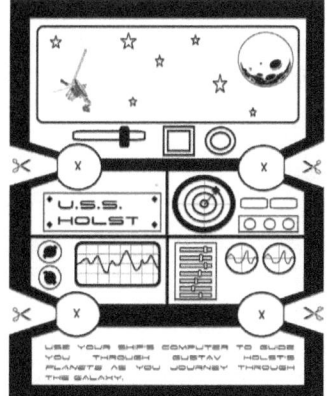

Figure 5.16 **Mission Control Main Template.** *Source*: Author

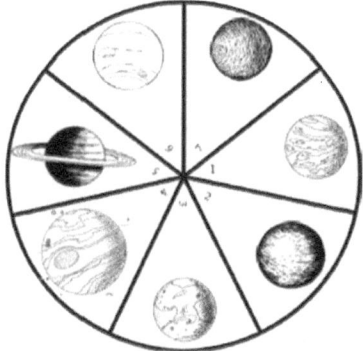

Figure 5.17 **Mission Control Planets Template.** *Source*: Author

Figure 5.18 **Mission Control Planets Template.** *Source*: Author

128   Chapter 5

The titles of the movements in Gustav Holst's *The Planets* are:
Mercury, The Winged Messenger
Venus, The Bringer of Peace
Mars, The Bringer of War
Jupiter, The Bringer of Jollity
Saturn, The Bringer of Old Age
Uranus, The Magician
Neptune, The Mystic Mission Control Circle Templates

Figure 5.19   Mission Control Planets Template. *Source*: Author

The style markings for each planet are:

Mercury: *Vivace*, or quick and lively
Venus: *Adagio*, or slow
Mars: *Allegro*, or quick
Jupiter: *Maestoso*, or majestically
Saturn: *Adagio*
Uranus: *Andante*, or moderately fast
Neptune: *Allegro*

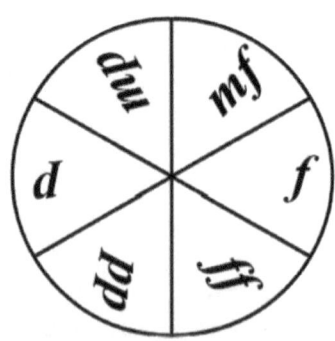

Figure 5.20   Mission Control Planets Template. *Source*: Author

Composers use Italian words and abbreviations to tell performers how loud or soft the music should be. In music, the word for how loud or quiet something should be is *dynamics*. Dynamics markings start with two Italian root words: *forte*, meaning loud, and *piano*, meaning soft or quiet. When the prefix *mezzo*, or medium, is added to the beginning of the words, we get *mezzoforte*, or medium loud, and *mezzopiano*, or medium soft. When the suffix *issimo*, or very, is added to the end of root words, we get *fortissimo*, or very loud, and *pianissimo*, or very soft.

Composers print abbreviations of these words on the music to tell the performer how loud or soft to make the music. The abbreviations for these words, in order from softest to loudest is:

Pianissimo	very soft	*pp*
Piano	soft	*p*
Mezzopiano	medium soft	*mp*
Mezzoforte	medium loud	*mf*
Forte	loud	*f*
Fortissimo	very loud	*ff*

ERIC CARLE SOLAR SYSTEM

Figure 5.21 Eric Carle Solar System Complete. *Source*: Author

Overview

For this project campers will create a solar system in the artistic style of Eric Carle. This project takes at least two days to complete. On the first day, introduce the project, and allow time for campers to paint their designs of each planet. On the second day, campers will cut out the planets, glue them onto black paper, and add finishing details.

Materials Needed

- Sample Eric Carle artwork
- Photographs or pictures of each planet
- Tempura paints (red, yellow, brown or tan, orange, white, green, blue, gray)
- Paint cups or bowls
- Paint brushes
- White paper
- Black construction paper (18" x 22")
- Scissors
- Glue
- Star stickers (optional)

Prepare

Cut white paper into 4-inch squares, enough for each camper to have 10 squares (9 planets plus the sun). Pour paint into bowls, add a paint brush to each bowl, and distribute one of each color to each table or painting station.

Teaching Sequence

First, introduce campers to the artwork of Eric Carle by showing any one of his books and discussing his painting technique. Eric Carle knew the basic colors and shapes of the object he wanted to paint, and began by paining color swirls and strokes on paper, experimenting with blends of different colors, varying brush strokes, and other techniques. Once this was dry, Mr. Carle cut shapes from his colored paper to assemble into the images he wanted to create.

Next, show some pictures of the planets in the solar system and invite campers imagine how Eric Carle might paint the planets as swirls of colors or brush strokes. Show a completed example of the Solar System activity, comparing the paintings of the planets to the photographs, and invite campers to identify each planet on the painting.

Distribute the squares of white paper (10 per camper). On one side of each square, ask campers to write their name, and the name of one planet (or the sun). On the other side, campers paint each square with color swirls, brush strokes, and other designs, using only the colors that they see in the planet. Once campers have painted all ten squares, set them aside to dry, and move on to the next Connections activity.

On the next day, distribute a sheet of black paper to each camper, ask campers to find their painted squares, and have a seat. Spend a few minutes discussing the sizes of the planets and the sun, and ask campers to arrange their squares in order from biggest planet to smallest. The planets in order from largest to smallest are Sun (biggest circle), Jupiter, Saturn, Uranus, Neptune, Earth, Venus, Mars, Mercury, and Pluto.

Have campers cut circles from each square, with the largest circle (the sun) at four inches in diameter, and the smallest circle (Pluto) about one inch in diameter. Although planets will not be cut to scale, it is helpful to talk about planet sizes and cut out the circles accordingly.

Ask campers to glue their planets to the black paper, in order from the sun (Mercury, Venus, Earth, Mars, Jupiter, Saturn, Uranus, Neptune, Pluto). Finally, invite campers to consider what else they might see in space (Saturn's rings, stars, asteroids, or satellites), and add extra details as desired.

ALIEN/AFRICAN MASKS

Materials Needed

Figure 5.22 Alien Mask Complete A. *Source*: Author

- Alien mask templates (see pages 134–135)
- Craft foam sheets (12" x 18") assorted colors
- Google eyes (medium to large)
- Construction paper (assorted colors)
- Scissors
- Hot glue
- Craft glue
- Small-hole punch
- Pencils
- White (scrap) paper
- Optional items to decorate the masks: craft feathers, craft beads, pipe cleaners, fabric or puff paint (tempura paint also works), markers

132 *Chapter 5*

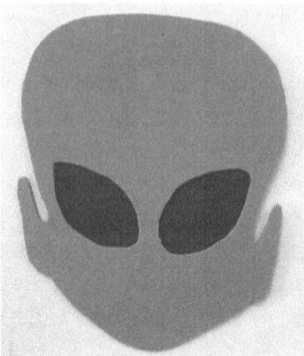

Figure 5.23 Alien Mask Complete B. *Source*: Author

Prepare

Cut the craft foam sheets into fourths (6" x 9") so that each sheet yields four masks. Cut out two of each alien mask template on thick card-stock paper

Figure 5.24 Alien Mask Complete C. *Source*: Author

Figure 5.25 Alien Mask Complete D. *Source*: Author

or file folder. Use an Internet search or other resource to find examples of African masks to use as models for the campers.

Teaching Sequence

Introduce campers to African masks. Throughout Africa, masks are used to tell stories, are worn in ceremonies or dances, are used to represent kings, gods, or ancestors, and for many other purposes. As you show a few examples, call attention to the intricate details of each mask, and invite campers to share their observations.

Next, show examples of the alien masks and lead a brief discussion about the differences in alien faces and people faces. Get campers to think creatively about how they will design their own alien mask.

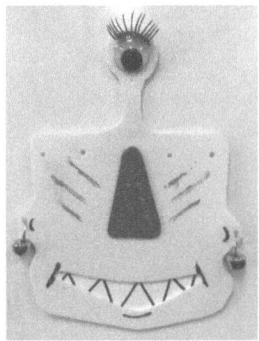

Figure 5.26   Alien Mask Complete E. *Source*: Author

Distribute a sheet of white paper and a pencil to each camper. Have campers trace one of the provided templates, or design their own alien mask, and sketch what they will want their alien to look like. Encourage campers to add a lot of detail and plan exactly what they will want their mask to look like before they begin making their final version. When campers have finished their first draft, distribute the supplies to have them construct their masks.

Alien Mask Templates

Printed dimensions of each mask should be no more than 9" (h) x 6" (w).
   Copy templates onto card-stock paper or file folder for campers to trace.

Figure 5.27 Alien Mask Template A. *Source*: Author

Figure 5.28 Alien Mask Template B. *Source*: Author

Figure 5.29 Alien Mask Template C. *Source*: Author

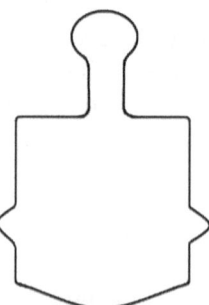

Figure 5.30 Alien Mask Template D. *Source*: Author

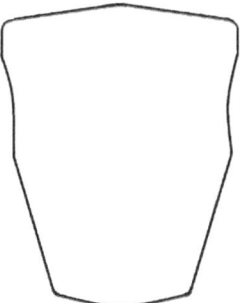

Figure 5.31 Alien Mask Template E. *Source*: Author

REMAINING TIME PROJECT EXTENSION ACTIVITY (OPTIONAL)

Materials Needed

- Nine white paper hanging Chinese lanterns of various sizes
- Tempura paints and brushes
- Pictures of each planet
- A way for the Chinese lanterns to light up (optional)

Overview

The purpose of this project is to have something for campers to do who finish their regular Connections projects before other campers. This project may also be used to provide extra decorations for the stage during the closing ceremony. Be sure campers have thoroughly completed their regular projects before they are allowed to work on the extra project.

Sequence

Use paints and brushes from the Eric Carle Solar System project to paint the Chinese lanterns like the planets in the solar system. When they are completed, hang them to dry, and then hang them over the stage or performance area during the closing ceremony.

Chapter 6

Games

This section contains instructions and equipment lists for game time. Game time should be held in a large room or gymnasium. For the games, you will need equipment that is readily available from physical education supply catalogs or websites (cones, beanbags, floor scooters, Poly Spots, etc.).

Consider purchasing equipment with income from registration, borrowing equipment from a local school, or making modifications to the games so that they can be played without equipment that may not be available to you. Some of the games also use small, handheld percussion instruments that may be borrowed from your camp's instruments Basics class.

The instructional components of many of the games require a set of matching cards on various music topics. You can either make your own matching cards, or purchase commercially made cards from music education suppliers. For the games in this book, choose between any one or more of the following options:

Rhythms

- A set of cards matching notes to note names
- A set of cards matching notes to Kodály, or other rhythmic syllables
- A set of one-measure rhythm cards matching notes to rhythm syllables

Music Symbols

- A set of cards matching music symbol with name or function

Staff Spelling

- A set of cards matching notes on a treble staff with letter name
- A set of cards matching words with notes on a treble staff that spell the words

Solfège

- A set of cards matching solfège syllable to hand sign
- A set of cards matching short melodic patterns on a treble staff to solfège syllables

Instruments

- A set of cards matching instrument picture to instrument name
- A set of cards matching instrument to instrument family (by name or by picture)

Composers

- A set of cards matching composer picture with name
- A set of cards matching composer facts to picture or name

GAME SCHEDULE AND ROTATION

The amount of time it takes to play a game is approximated below, and may fluctuate based on the size of your program, and other factors. The game director should set out and prepare equipment in advance, including equipment for an extra game if the scheduled games are completed earlier than anticipated.

Day One

- Life Raft *(20 minutes)*
- Transition/setup (2–5 minutes)
- Moon Rocks *(20 minutes)*
- Jingle Ninja *(time permitting)*

Day Two

- Tether Tug *(10–15 minutes)*
- Transition/setup (2–5 minutes)

- Rondo Relay *(10–15 minutes)*
- Transition/setup (2–5 minutes)
- The Navigator *(10–15 minutes)*

Day Three

- Space Station *(10–15 minutes)*
- Transition/setup (2–5 minutes)
- The Navigator *(10–15 minutes)*
- Transition / setup (2–5 minutes)
- Jingle Bell Roll *(10–15 minutes)*
- Jingle Ninja or review a game from day one or two *(time permitting)*

Day Four

- Danger Zone *(10–15 minutes)*
- Transition/setup (2–5 minutes)
- Theme and Variations Relay *(10–15 minutes)*
- Transition/setup (2–5 minutes)
- Spelling Bee Relay or Egg Scramble *(10–15 minutes)*
- Caterpillar Relay *(time permitting)*

Day Five

Voter's Choice game time. Early in the day, the game director should allow campers to vote on their favorite game and play the games that receive the top two or three votes.

SCORE SHEET TEMPLATE

Use this score sheet as a template to keep track of team points during game time.

- First place = 100 points
- Second place = 75 points
- Third place = 50 points
- Fourth place = 25 points

Additional points may be awarded for sportsmanship, being the first team quiet, being the first team lined up, and other incentives.

Table 6.1 Game Time Score Sheet

Activity	Red	Blue	Yellow	Green
Daily Total				

DAY ONE

Life Raft

Materials Needed

- Floor scooter for each team (available from PE and education supply catalogs)
- Long rope for each team
- Cones or other way to mark team lines and starting/stopping points
- A pair of oven mitts for each team (optional)

Setup

Teams line up at one end of the playing area. Place a scooter and pair of oven mitts at the front of each team line. Tie one end of the rope to the back of the scooter so that the team can retrieve it by pulling it back to the team line. Place a cone or team marker for each team at the other end of the playing area, directly across from each team line.

Introduction

The scenario for Life Raft is that each team's spacecraft has broken and they have to get across the field of toxic sludge (the middle of the playing area) to the rescue ship at the other side, without touching the floor.

Play

The first player on each team sits on the scooter and uses his/her hands to push the scooter along the floor, wearing oven mitts as protection against the toxic sludge. When the first player reaches the other end, he/she gets off, places the oven mitts on the scooter, and the team pulls the scooter and oven mitts back to the team line for the next player to use. Play continues until all players have reached the other end.

If one oven mitt falls off while the scooter is being pulled back to the team line, the next player may only use one hand, and must scoot to rescue the fallen mitt before reaching the other side. If both oven mitts fall off on the return trip, the player must run back to rejoin the team.

Options

Emergency Rescue. Spread cards around the playing area for campers to rescue as they roll to the other side. For this option, any number of cards may be used to teach or assess a variety of music content. Some examples include:

- Use instrument cards and assign one instrument family per team. Players must scoot around until they find an instrument in their family, and take the instrument to the other side of the playing area.
- Use rhythm or pitch cards so that players collect the notes to spell a designated rhythm or melody.

Asteroids. Spread Poly Spots or cones around the playing surface. The Poly Spots are asteroids and players must navigate through the playing area without touching an asteroid. Any camper who accidentally rolls into an asteroid must go back to the team line, give the scooter to the next team player, and have another turn later.

Asteroids (version 2). Spread Poly Spots or cones around the playing surface and place cards under each asteroid. Campers will approach an asteroid, pick it up, and rescue the card (take it back to their team line). The winning team is the first team to rescue all of its cards.

Under some Poly Spots, place a card labeled *CRASH*. If a player picks up this Poly Spot, he/she has to return to the team line, give the scooter to the next player in line, and have another turn later (the *CRASH* card goes back under the Poly Spot, campers have to remember where they are to avoid picking them up again).

Moon Rocks

Materials Needed

- Painters tape to mark floor
- One hula hoop for each team
- Cards (instruments, rhythm, composer, etc.) or beanbags

Setup

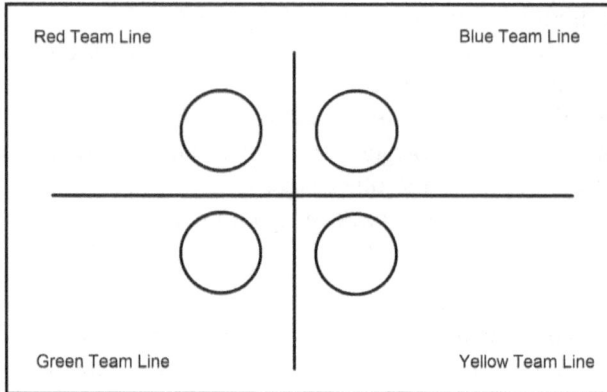

Figure 6.1 Moon Rocks. *Source*: Author.

Have teams line up with one line in each corner of the playing area. Use painter's tape to divide the playing surface floor into four quadrants. Place a hula hoop on the floor in each team's quadrant. Determine what kinds of cards you will use for play, and spread cards (moon rocks) out all over the floor, in no particular order, ensuring that there are no cards in the hula hoops.

Play

The first player from each team runs into the playing area, grabs a card that his/her team needs and places it in the team's hula hoop before running back to the team line for the next player to have a turn. Team members can go anywhere in the room to get a card, but may be tagged if they leave their quadrant.

Each player can perform only one task before returning to the team line. For instance, a player may choose to get a card and then return to the team line; or a player may choose to tag a player from another team who is attempting to take a card from his/her quadrant. Once a player has retrieved a card or tagged a player, he/she has to return to the team line.

Play continues for a set period of time, either until one team has a predetermined number of cards or for a set number of minutes and the team with the most cards is the winner.

Jingle Ninja

Materials Needed

- Egg shakers, small instruments, or items that make noise when moved
- Jingle bracelets (enough for one player from each team to wear 2 to 4 bracelets)

- Blindfolds (enough for one player per team)
- Cones or other items to mark team lines

Setup

Players line up in teams at one end of the playing area. The first player on each team puts a jingle bracelet on each wrist and ankle. Another player *(the Guardian)* is blindfolded and taken to sit at the other end of the playing area, facing the teams, and with a number of noise makers on the floor within arm's reach.

Play

At the starting signal, the first player from each team (wearing jingle bracelets) runs to the other end of the playing area where the Guardians await. Once the player reaches the other end, he/she moves as slowly and quietly as possible, trying to steal an instrument from an opposing team's Guardian without making a sound. The Guardian listens carefully and attempts to touch(tag) the player stealing the instrument.

Players may not steal instruments from their own team's Guardian. The Guardian may not get up or move, and may only tag players within arm's reach. If a player is able to get an instrument without being tagged, he/she takes the instrument back to the team. If a player is tagged, he/she returns to the team empty-handed, and helps put the jingle bracelets on the next player who then tries to steal an instrument.

Sometimes, players spend an excessive amount of time trying to get to the instruments without being tagged by the Guardian. You may wish to enforce a five-second rule where students have five seconds after they cross a certain point to attempt to grab an instrument before they have to return to the team line.

The winning team can be determined as the team with the most instruments by a predesignated amount of time, or as the first team to retrieve a predesignated number of instruments.

DAY TWO

Tether Tug

Materials needed

- Floor scooter for each team
- Long rope for each team (long enough to reach from one end of the playing surface to the other)

- Cones or other way to mark team lines and starting/stopping points
- Cards, small instruments, or other items for campers to retrieve (optional)

Setup

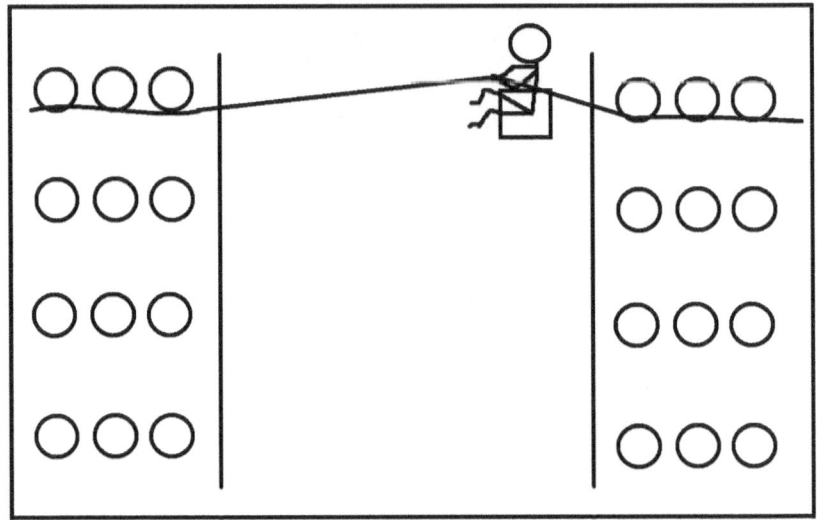

Figure 6.2 Tether Tug. *Source*: Author.

Divide each team into two equal groups and arrange team lines so that half of the team is at one end of the playing area, and the second half is at the other end. Stretch out the ropes for each team so that every player can grab onto the rope. Place a floor scooter at the starting point for each team line.

Introduction

A tether is the cable used to attach astronauts to the spaceship. Without it, they would float away into space. Whenever astronauts leave the spaceships, they tether (tie) themselves to the ship so that they can get back.

Play

The first player for each team sits on the scooter. The players at the other end of the gym hold onto the rope but do not pull. At the starting signal, the player pulls himself/herself across the floor using the rope until he reaches the other half of his team.

At this point, the player gets off the scooter and joins his/her teammates. One player from this side of the room then gets on the scooter and pulls himself to the other side. Play continues until all team members have switched sides. The winner is the first team to switch sides.

Option. Turn Tether Tug into a matching game where each team has some cards on one end of the playing area and matching cards on the other. Players have to take a card (only one at a time) from one end to the other to find its match. In this version of play, the game ends when a team has found matches to all its cards.

For safety reasons, be sure that team members who are holding onto the rope do not pull. The player sitting on the scooter pulls himself/herself across the room.

Rondo Relay

Materials needed

- Poly Spots (floor spot markers)
- Beanbags
- Cones or other way to mark team lines
- Miscellaneous points in the playing area

Setup

Teams line up at one end of the playing area. Spread objects (team-colored cones, Poly Spots, or beanbags) around the playing surface.

Introduction

Campers will need a brief bit of introduction to Rondo Form (A B A C A). As an introductory lesson, have campers listen to Beethoven's *Rondo a Capriccio* as you lead them in nonlocomotor movements that represent the form.

Play

Option 1. The first five players in each line will run in the first round, the next group in the second round, and so on. At the starting signal, the first five players will go to the cone at the other end of the playing area and back, one at a time, in rondo form. Each player has to remember what previous players have done so they can either recreate the movement, or avoid recreating it. For example,

- Player 1: runs (A)
- Player 2: skips (B)
- Player 3: has to remember to run (A)
- Player 4: has to remember not to skip or run, and may run backward or something different (C)
- Player 5: has to remember to run (A)

A player who performs an incorrect movement has to return to the starting line and go again. The winning team is the first team in each round with all five players back across the team line. As play continues, you might make scooters or other items available for use (hula hoops, jump ropes, etc.). You might also choose to make certain movements off-limits so that campers will not be able to do the same thing over and over.

With smaller teams, use a three-part rondo instead of five for this and all other options.

Option 2. Randomly spread Poly Spots around the playing area, ensuring that there are at least four or five spots for each team. At the starting signal, the first player runs to a Poly Spot of his/her team's color (point A), then to another spot (point B), then back to A (the first spot), then to a new spot (C), then back to A (the first spot), and then back to the team line to tag the next player.

Team members must watch carefully to remember the exact spots that were used, and the order in which they come. Play continues until all team members have run the rondo and the winner is the first team with all players back on the team lines. With each new round of play, ensure that each team has a different starting player and that a different rondo pattern is chose.

The game director may choose to preselect each teams' rondo rather than allowing the first team player to choose his/her own route. The game director may also choose to mark each team's route, or may determine something for players to do who goes to an incorrect spot, or goes to the spots out of order (return to the team line and start over, do 5 jumping jacks before continuing, etc.).

Option 3. The third and final option is similar to option two, but increases in complexity as the rondo develops. At the starting signal, the first player runs to a Poly Spot (point A), and then back to the team line. The second player runs to point A, and then to a new Poly Spot (point B), and then back to the team line. The third player runs to point A, then to point B, then back to point A before returning to the team line. The next player retraces these steps, and then runs to a new Poly Spot (point C) before returning to the team line. The fifth and final player retraces the path of player four, then goes back to point A to complete the rondo before returning to the team line.

The Navigator

Materials needed

- One blindfold per team
- Assorted collection of handheld non-pitched percussion instruments
- Scooter for each team (optional)

Setup

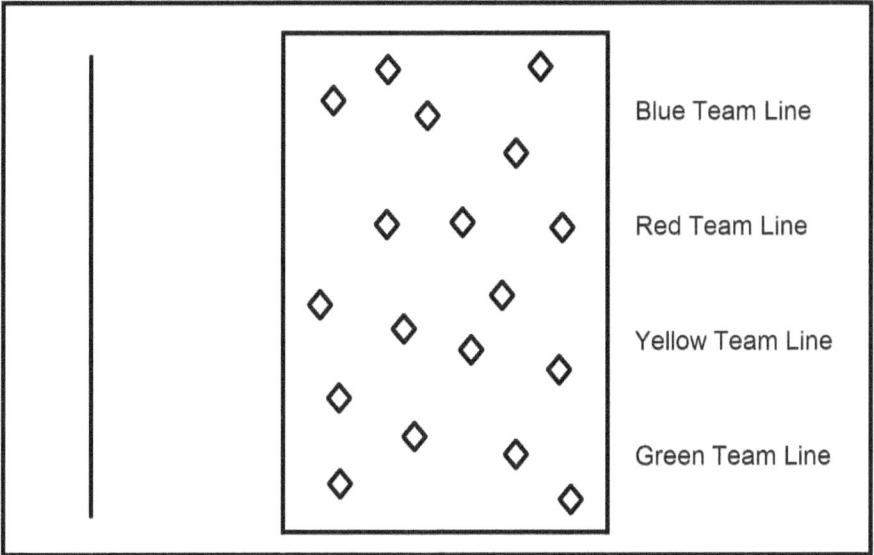

Figure 6.3 Navigator. *Source*: Author.

Teams line up at one end of the playing area. In front of each team line, place a blindfold, a handheld percussion instrument and, a scooter (optional). Place a cone or team marker for each team at the other end of the playing area, directly across from each team line. Randomly spread Poly Spots (asteroids) throughout the center of the playing area.

Introduction

Ask campers to imagine that their spacecraft has crashed on a dangerous planet and they have to navigate through the asteroid belt to safety; but to get through the asteroid belt, they can only use their ears.

Play

The first player from each team (the *pilot*) puts on the blindfold and sits down on the scooter. The second player (the *guide*) selects an instrument to lead the pilot through the asteroid field. At the starting signal, the guide plays the instrument for the blindfolded pilot to follow. The pilot follows the guide through the asteroid belt, to safety on the other side.

The guide may only play the instrument and may not touch the pilot or use his/her voice to navigate the pilot. If a pilot touches an asteroid, he/she has to start over. Once the team safely reaches the other side, the pilot stays put and the guide takes the scooter back to the team line and becomes the new pilot. For the last rotation, the first pilot becomes the guide for the last player. The winning team is first team with all players across the asteroid belt.

DAY THREE

Space Station

This is a game of many games in which teams play one game or complete one task, and then rotate to the next station where they will complete the next task. Teams accumulate points in each task, and the team with the most points at the conclusion of all tasks is the winner.

The number of games or stations is determined by the size of your program and the amount of time allotted for Space Station. Usually, three to four games are selected from the five below (one station per team), and one game is selected as the *pacer*, or the game that determines how much time each team has to complete their task.

Set up the playing area into the number of stations or activities you plan to use and have teams rotate through activity stations.
Example:

Activity 1 (Pacer): Buddy Walkers / Blue team
Activity 2: Endless Rain Stick Red team
Activity 3: Ring Around the Rosie Green team

The red and green teams accumulate points for the number of times they can complete their tasks in the amount of time it takes the blue team to complete the buddy walk. When the blue team completes the buddy walk, tabulate points for the red and green teams, and then rotate so that each team is at a new station and the new team on the buddy walkers sets the pace.

Beanbag Toss

Materials needed

- Rhythm target (drawn on butcher paper, posterboard, canvas, or shower curtain liner)
  Whole note = center (bullseye) 4 points
  Half notes = next circle 2 points

Quarter notes = next circle 1 point
Eighth notes = next circle ½ point
- Beanbag
- Stopwatch (or a way to keep track of time limit)

Setup

Lay the target on the ground and set a mark a few feet back for players to line up. You may choose to make the mark closer for younger players, or those needing accommodations.

Play

Players line up behind the mark and throw the beanbag to the target to get as many points as possible. Once a player has thrown, he/she moves to the back of the line for the next player to take a turn. Teams continue to accumulate points until the Pacer team finishes its task.

Buddy Walkers

In Space Stations, *Buddy Walkers* is one of the pacer activities that is used to determine how much time other teams have to complete their tasks.

Materials needed

- Buddy walkers (available in physical education supply catalogs)
- Cones to mark start and stop points

Setup

Divide the pacer team into two groups. Place one half of the team at one end of the playing area, and the second half at the other.

Play

At the starting signal, two members step on the buddy walkers and attempt to walk from one side of the playing area to the other where the second half of their team is waiting. When they reach the other side, they give the buddy walkers to two other members of their team who walk the buddy walkers back. This back and forth relay continues until all team members have switched sides.

    A steady beat of some kind will help players as they learn to master the buddy walkers. Encourage players to count a steady beat and/or sing a selected song to help them march together with the steady beat.

Jack Be Quick

In Space Stations, *Jack Be Quick* is one of the pacers that is used to determine how much time other teams have to complete their tasks.

Materials needed

- 4-Square ball
- Cones to mark team line
- Matching cards or other items for players to retrieve.

Setup

The pacer team lines up at one end of the playing area. Spread out a large number of objects (cards, beanbags, or small instruments) for players to retrieve.

Play

At the start of the game, the first player runs with the ball into the playing area. The player bounces the ball and then attempts to pick up an object before the ball hits the ground again. The player catches the ball and takes the ball and object back to the team. The ball is given to the second player who goes in for a turn. This continues until all items have been retrieved. If the ball touches the ground a second time, the player must put the object back on the ground, and run the ball to the next player for their turn.

Variations. The objects for players to retrieve can vary based on instructional needs. As the pacer activity in Space Stations, have players retrieve beanbags or something simple. If you are using this as an independent game, have players retrieve matching cards that are used in Danger Zone and Junk Yard Dog.

Endless Rain Stick

Materials needed
- Egg- shaker maraca for each team (ping-pong balls also work)
- Maraca slide for each player (one Boomwhacker for each team member, or wrapping paper tube or paper-towel tube)

Setup

Have team members stand in a circle, and distribute a maraca slide to each team member. One player places the egg shaker in his/her tube.

Play

At the starting signal, the first player tilts his/her tube toward his neighbor so the egg shaker rolls down the tube. The neighbor attempts to catch the egg shaker in his/her tube and then tilts his/her tube toward his/her other neighbor. This continues around the circle. If a player drops the egg, he/she picks it up, places it back in his/her tube, and continues to pass to the next player.

Ring Around the Rosie

Materials needed

Hula hoop for each team
Stopwatch (or a way to keep track of time limit)

Setup

Each team stands in a circle, holding hands. The hula hoop is hung around the arm of one player. This player is designated as the starting point.

Play

At the starting signal, players pass the hula hoop around the circle without letting go of their neighbor's hands (players have to step through the hula hoop to get it from the left side of their body to the right, and keep it moving around the circle). The team earns one point for each time the hula hoop gets all the way around the team circle in the allotted time.

Jingle Bell Roll

Instructions for Jingle Bell Roll are available in *Essential Listening Activities for the Music Classroom* (2008), by Eric Branscome. Available from Alfred Music.

DAY FOUR

Danger Zone

Materials needed

- Cones to mark team lines and "danger zone"
- Objects for players to match (see variations below)
- Dodge balls or playground balls
- Floor scooters (optional)

Setup

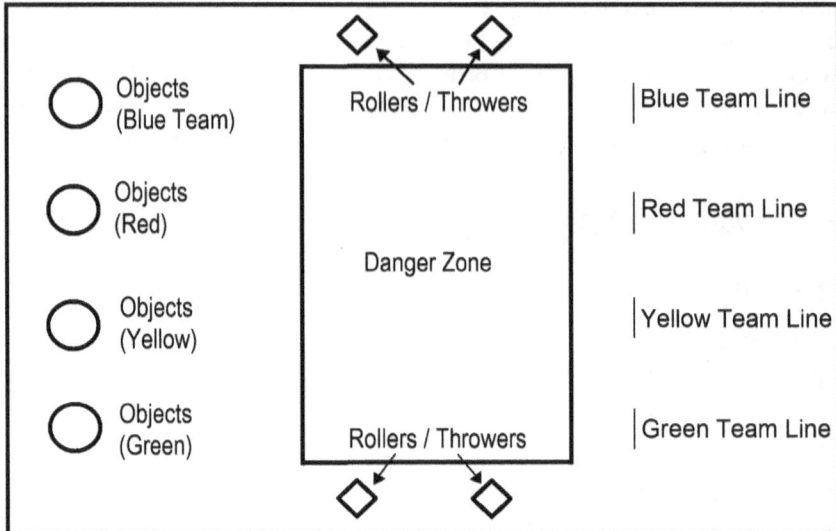

Figure 6.4   Danger Zone Set-Up.

Players, divided into two to four teams, line up behind cones at one end of the playing area. Place objects for players to retrieve at the other end of the playing area. Use additional cones to mark off an area in the middle of the playing area as the "danger zone" (make sure players have to run through the danger zone to get to the objects). Select one to two leaders or interns to be rollers for each round. Rollers stand on the left and right sides of the danger zone (it is helpful to have an equal number of rollers on the left and right sides of the danger zone [two or so on each side]).

Play

At the starting signal, the first player from each team tries to run through the danger zone to reach the objects at the other end of the playing area, and bring one object back to the team. Rollers attempt to get players out by rolling dodge balls at the runners only when they have entered the danger zone. If a player is hit, he/she must turn around and go back to the team for the next player in line to go. Rollers may not enter the danger zone except to retrieve a ball, but then must exit the danger zone before they can roll again.

If a player has already retrieved an object and is hit in the danger zone during the return run, he/she must place the object on the ground where he/she was hit and return to the team. Players can only be hit when they are in the danger zone.

The next player may attempt to retrieve the object in addition to getting another object from the stack at the other end of the playing area. Play continues until a team has retrieved all objects from the other end of the playing area OR until the end of a predetermined amount of time. See variations below for more information.

Variations. The objects for players to retrieve can vary based on instructional needs. Suggestions include:

- **Rhythms Cards:** At the start of the game, post (or clap) a rhythm that teams must spell by retrieving the correct notes and rests. To win, teams must not only retrieve the correct notes/rests, but must also place them in the correct order at the front of their team line.
- **Staff Spelling Cards:** At the start of the game, post or say a word that teams must spell by retrieving the correct notes. To win, teams must not only retrieve the correct notes/rests, but must also place them in the correct order at the front of their team line.
- **Instruments:** Have instrument pictures on cards at the opposite end of the playing area, and instrument names listed on a large sheet of paper or poster board at the front of team lines. Players retrieve an instrument and match each picture with the correct name before the next player can go. The winner is the first team with a completed ensemble (jazz band, orchestra, band, etc.) or instrument family.
- **Composers or Performers:** Have composer pictures on cards at the opposite end of the playing area, and composer names listed on a large sheet of paper or poster board at the front of team lines. Players must match picture with name similarly to the instrument option listed above.
- **Music Symbols:** Have music symbols on cards at the end of the playing area, and composer names listed on a large sheet of paper or poster board at the front of team lines. Players must match picture with name similarly to the instrument option listed above.

Theme and Variations Relay

Materials Needed

- Cones or other way to mark team lines and starting/stopping points
- Cones or other way to mark a spot at the other end of the playing area for each team
- Floor scooters, hula hoops, or other items for teams to use (optional)

Setup

Teams line up at one end of the playing area. Place a pile of beanbags, cones, Poly Spots at the front of each team line. Place a cone or team marker for each team at the other end of the playing area, directly across from each team line.

Introduction

Campers will need a brief bit of introduction to Theme and Variation Form. Play a recording of the second movement of Haydn's *Surprise Symphony* to listen for the theme and the ways the composer changed it each time it repeated.

Play

The first three to five players in each line will run in the first round, the next group in the second round, and so on. At the starting signal, the first five players will go to the cone at the other end of the playing area and back, one at a time, in theme and variations form. The game director will provide a theme. The first player simply performs the theme and each of the next players has to do something different, still using the theme.

Suggested Themes

- Run: the first player runs, the next players have to change something about the way they run
- Scooter: players have to find unique, creative ways to ride (or not ride) the scooter
- Hula hoop (wearing, rolling, scooting, spinning, etc.)
- Ball (rolling, bouncing, throwing, kicking, etc.)
- Animal motions
- Others (see how creative you can get)

Spelling Bee Relay

Note: This game requires a certain level of musical literacy that some students may not have acquired. It is helpful to begin this game with a brief time of instruction to teach the names of the lines and spaces in the treble clef staff. You may also wish to create "cheat sheets" to help younger players, or players with minimal music reading experience. As you play this game, you may also wish to create your own set of rules for how older campers can help younger campers who have not yet been taught how to read notes in the staff.

Materials needed

- Large music staves marked on the floor (sidewalk chalk for outdoor play, or painter's tape for indoor play)

- Cones to mark team or player lines
- Beanbags or other object for players to use as notes
- A list of words that can be spelled using the 7 letters of the music alphabet

Table 6.2 Music Alphabet Word Bank

ace	badge	beg	dad	face
add	bag	begged	deaf	fad
added	baggage	cab	decade	fade
age	bead	cabbage	deed	faded
bad	bed	cafe	deface	fed
badge	bee	cage	edge	fee
bag	beef	dab	egg	feed

Setup

Teams should line up at one end of the playing area. Mark large staves on the floor at the other end of the playing area (one staff member per team). Place the beanbags (or other objects) in the middle of the playing area.

Play

Begin by announcing a word that can be spelled with the letters of the music alphabet. At the starting signal the first player on each team runs to retrieve a beanbag, and takes the beanbag to the staff. At the staff, the player places the beanbag on the correct line or space of the first letter of the given word. The player then runs back to the team for the second player to go. The second player places the second letter and so on until the entire word is spelled correctly.

If a player places a letter in an incorrect line or space, the next player should correct the letter instead of placing a new beanbag. The winner is the first team to correctly spell the word and return to the team line. Not every player will run in each round, depending on the number of players in each team and the number of letters in each word.

Word Bank. These words can be spelled with the seven letters of the musical alphabet.

EGG SCRAMBLE

Materials needed

- A large number of Easter eggs (100–150)
- Items to fill Easter eggs (pennies, marbles, plastic craft beads, rice)
- There should be identical numbers of eggs in each group.

Setup

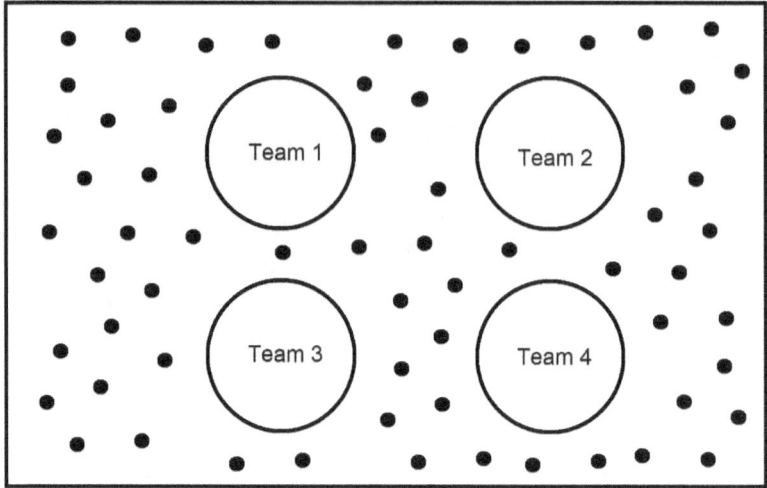

Figure 6.5 *Egg Scramble.* *Source*: Author.

Easter eggs should be filled and spread all over the playing surface. Teams sit in individual team circles. One person in each team is chosen as the staring player (teams will start with this person and continue around the circle to the right).

Play (Round One)

At the starting signal, the first player in each team runs to get an egg and brings it back to his/her team. Team members pass the egg around the circle as quickly as possible, for each team member to shake the egg and determine what is inside.

After the egg has made its way around the team circle, the team places the egg in the middle of the circle, and the next player runs to retrieve an egg. As more and more eggs are collected and passed around the circle, team members must work together to sort their eggs by sound and put eggs in the correct piles. Once all eggs have been collected, teams receive one point for each egg in the correct pile.

At the end of the game, encourage discussion about the contents of the eggs and how each object sounds different inside the eggs. Once all eggs have been counted, have players spread the eggs back out on the playing surface floor and return to their circles.

Play (Round Two)

Round two of play is identical to the first round except that now, players know what is in the eggs and each team is assigned to only retrieve one type of egg. For example, team one will look for eggs with pennies, and team two will look for eggs with plastic craft beads.

At the starting signal, the first player from each team runs to the end of the gym, picks up and egg and listens for what is inside. Players may only shake one egg before returning to the team circle. If the egg contains correct sound, the player returns to the team circle with the egg. If it is not the correct sound, the player returns the egg to the floor and runs back to the team circle.

The next player then runs to shake and egg, and so on. The winning team is the first team to retrieve ten eggs with the correct sound, or the team with the most eggs at a predetermined amount of time.

Caterpillar Relay

Materials needed

- Cones to mark team lines
- One set of matching cards for each team (use any of the matching card variations listed in the Games introduction)

Setup

Teams line up relay style, with legs spread at shoulder width. One half of matching cards is placed at the back of each team, and the other half at the front.

Play

At the starting signal, the player in the back of the line takes a card from the stack in the back and crawls through the legs of his/her team. When the player reaches the front of the line, he/she places the card next to the correct matching card in the front. The player then returns to the front of the team line. The new player in back then grabs the next card and continues play as before.

Play continues until all players have crawled through the line or until all cards have been taken from the back to the front. The winning team is the first team to match all their items, or the team with the most matches at the end of a predetermined period of time.

DAY FIVE

Voter's Choice: At the beginning of the day, allow students to vote on their favorite game and play the games that receive the top two or three votes.

www.ingramcontent.com/pod-product-compliance
Lightning Source LLC
Chambersburg PA
CBHW031553300426
44111CB00006BA/296